Nothing
Divine Dies:

The Poetry of Nature

Vita Brevis Poetry Anthology, Volume III
Compiled and Edited
By Vita Brevis Press

Table of Contents

"Nothing divine dies. All good is eternally reproductive. The beauty of nature reforms itself in the mind, and not for barren contemplation, but for new creation."

– Ralph Waldo Emerson, Nature

Self-Portrait as Root - Robert Okaji

My full beauty lies beneath sight,
spread below in dark anchorage,
the heft of a life lived in the
underside, thriving in cause and
bound to earth. What is love if not
the slow sip of nutrients rising? I
grip and expand, maintain and
absorb, securing place with
steadiness. From me, you grow.
Follow this thought and return
to its seed near the surface. I am
truth, unhindered. Light, reversed.

Robert Okaji is a half-Japanese Texan seeking work in Indiana. His poetry has appeared or is forthcoming in riverSedge, Tipton Poetry Review, Clade Song, MockingHeart Review, Vox Populi, Genuine Gold and elsewhere.

Age - Sandra Salinas Newton

The oak, the elm, the birch, the juniper and yew,
All age with grace and dignity;
Whether stark in snow or heavy in heat,
They know their majesty and wear it
With royal understanding.

We once admired the wood,
The trees that sheltered and succored us,
And we tried to imitate them
In the work of our hands and backs:
Strength and stability, solidity.

But then we turned our love to stone:
Implacable and ruthless, cold
And deep and thicker than ice.
So we toiled with hammer and chisel,
Sculpting our cities, our families and lives,
To the imitation of eternity.

Wood changes, bends, and flows with time,
Its grain the gentle story
Of breeze and rain and rich soil.
But rock remains and battles
The winds and storms and cracked earth.

Like stone, regret is hard;
In the soft boughs of wood
We can be redeemed.

Sandra Salinas Newton is a Filipina-American professor emeritus of English currently living in Austin, Texas. Her published work includes texts, fiction, and most recently, poetry. She is also working on a novel. Her website is snewton.net.

Grief - Cynthia Pitman

dedicated to Kevin Nagle

Outside, a smoke-brown hummingbird
flutters by the feeder,
then floats on the cold wind
to a spindly stick of a branch
strung sparse with wintered leaves
weathered in the gray San Francisco fog.
Inside, we mourn.

Cynthia Pitman has been published in Vita Brevis, Pain and Renewal, Brought to Sight & Swept Away, Amethyst Review, Ekphrastic Journal, Third Wednesday (One Sentence Poem finalist), Saw Palm (Pushcart Prize nominee), Red Fez (Story of the Week), and others. Her book, The White Room, was published in 2020 by Kelsay Books.

Garden Farewell - E.M. Epstein

If you leave a garden
Go in early fall
When you've harvested some of its bounty
But not all

Leave some tomatoes
Ripening on the vine
An eggplant in its purpling

So the new gardener
Will taste its sweetness
Know the fruits of your labors
See what's possible from this soil

Spring will come;
The work of tilling and weeding
Amending soil for the next seeding

Leave while the fullness fills your soul
And know that you were the steward here
But not the owner
That what you left behind
Is no more than a season's turning

E.M. Epstein is an editor who works with words every day, but she has never published a poem before. She lives in the Pacific Northwest. These poems were inspired by gardening and the resilience of nature, even in the time of climate change.

Survival - David Lee Garrison

In a gang with no apparent leader,
birds swirl down and light on the feeder,

plunge their beaks in seed and corn,
clasping wood and wire like thorns.

I startle them when I get up —
a shadow with a coffee cup —

but they return to dig in snow
and scavenge with the greedy crows

emerging from the honeysuckle.
Mourning doves make branches buckle.

Finding strength in numbers, finches,
wrens, and sparrows scratch for inches,

gobbling half their weight each day.
Survival only *looks* like play.

The poetry of David Lee Garrison has been published widely and read by Garrison Keillor on The Writer's Almanac. His new book is Light in the River (Dos Madres Press).

Bale - Joel Scarfe

A bale has broken free,
and is rolling down a gentle hill

where love was turned
before the clouds came in,

before the rain blew corn-stubble
into cracking the skin,

the eye, where the earth moves,
where the field is born,

the ear, where the barn owl's song
is indelibly torn.

Joel Scarfe's poems feature internationally in magazines, periodicals and anthologies including Black Lives Matter: Poems for a New World, and Brought to Sight and Swept Away. He lives in Bristol UK with the Danish ceramicist Rebecca Edelmann and their two children.

The First Whack of Light
- Mark Andrew Heathcote

As a boy, I loved verdant virgin lands
the first whack of light peeking through the mist
glistening-like a golden cloak sun-kissed
and nature's volume going through its radio bands
I loved wands of droplets weighted just so
the silent dew cannot enumerate
-watching robin redbreast reverberates
his shrill bloated song to what do we owe

-this honour of your presence little friend,
why does the earthworm turn tail with the snail?
Does your red jersey; scold their eyes, offend.
As one kingdom ascends upon the vale
-another descends blindly as a mole, a bat
lucky is I in my bright habitat.

Mark Andrew Heathcote is adult learning difficulties support worker, his poetry has been published in many journals, magazines and anthologies, he resides in the UK, from Manchester; he is the author of "In Perpetuity" and "Back on Earth" two books of poems published by a CTU publishing group, ~ Creative Talents Unleashed.

Gardening is Like a Prayer in Hope
- Megha Sood

As I bend down. Just as if I'm kneeling in the pew.
As sacred as a prayer to me, I start pulling out the weeds.
to make the home for my gorgeous lilies and bulbs of magnolias.
The dead makes way for the living.

Like a sacred offering to nature and a distraction for myself
Trying to disguise me like those puny twigs hiding.
Behind our flaws and scars.
Camouflaging is the sustenance for our soul.

I bend my knees with the burden of grief on my straight
shoulders,
Like a burgeoning moon, I bear scars on my soul.

Some days it is clear other days, they are eclipsed.
I'm pulling them out one by one as I count
the pain of those needles lodged in my soul

I say it to myself under the muted breath
"Gardening is like a prayer in hope"
I bend. Genuflect. As I start the next row.

Megha Sood is an Award-Winning Poet, Editor, Author, based in New Jersey, USA. Associate Editor at MookyChick(UK), Life and Legends (USA), and Literary Partner "Life in Quarantine" with Stanford University, USA. Chapbook ("My Body is Not an Apology", Finishing Line Press, 2021) and Full Length ("My Body Lives Like a Threat", FlowerSongPress,2021).

Backyard Morse Code - Suzanne Cottrell

I sit on our back deck,
Enjoy my morning cup of coffee.
Puffs of milky clouds
Decorate cerulean sky.
Sunlight glints through branches.
Scarlet cardinal perches
High on a water elm limb.
Its boisterous Morse Code of
Dot dash dot dash dot dash,
Not its usual melodious song of
Pretty, pretty, pretty.
What is its urgent message?
Predator nearby,
Plea for a mate,
Nestlings to feed,
I listen to its message,
Perhaps an SOS,
Fails to elicit a response.
Male cardinal flies off.
I stay, finish my coffee, wonder,
What was the message?

Suzanne Cottrell, an outdoor enthusiast and retired teacher, lives with her husband in rural Piedmont North Carolina. She is the author of three poetry chapbooks: Gifts of the Seasons, Autumn and Winter; Gifts of the Seasons, Spring and Summer; and Scarred Resilience.

Weeding - E.M. Epstein

It doesn't take much to imagine
A time when we might all be grateful for weeds
If chaos wins, and the world of neat gardens with plant life
hemmed in by bark dust gives way

Oxalis, shotweed, dandelion, horsetail

Learn their names

Think, as you dig and tear at their roots
(That still elude you, and spread)
About a time when you might be grateful for
Familiar greens in an unfamiliar world

Be amazed by their scattered seeds, rhizomes, tenaciousness
Even as you curse them for finding ways to grow out of every
crack
In your old concrete driveway

E.M. Epstein is an editor who works with words every day, but she has never published a poem before. She lives in the Pacific Northwest. These poems were inspired by gardening and the resilience of nature, even in the time of climate change.

autumn sunset - Kathryn Sadakierski

pink and copper skies,
rusty leaves ignite,
the smell of kettlecorn
like burnished gold,
tickling the hungry nose.

this evening is like a ghost
of the country fair,
like I never left,
like now,
instead of my backyard,
I'm there.

expectancy is in the sky
that patiently waits for stars,
twinkle lights
just starting to glow
in the horizon,
softened putty
of pastel clay,
molding the night's shape.

the whisper of cold
is in autumn's breath,
just smoke to wisp away;
we are warm in the knowledge of light,
still softening the sky,
the sun a rose
that hasn't lost its fragrance
or bloom of color,
pink and copper like dawn,
as though all endings could ever be
are beginnings.

Kathryn Sadakierski's writing has appeared in Critical Read, Halfway Down the Stairs, Literature Today, NewPages Blog, Northern New England Review, and elsewhere. Her micro-chapbook "Travels through New York" was published by Origami Poems Project (2020). She graduated summa cum laude with a B.A. and M.S. from Bay Path University.

Silently Lulled - Mark Andrew Heathcote

Falling leaves they're like parchment memories
they crisp stronger than ever was before.
Falling in your lap; change trajectories
hand clasping - the seed of the sycamore
and as it does in nature's store, the winds howl
the tree-bares-all. Naked autumn-fall
roots on-this-earth so deep, they groan and growl
never, wanting to lose an inch of, bedroll
but as all things collapse, so does - the mind
into its own-rich-black velvety mulch,
that resembles ourselves consigned
these amber pages, which drop-silently-lulled
we give up our evergreen fripperies
tongue and cheek our emerald mysteries.

Mark Andrew Heathcote is adult learning difficulties support worker, his poetry has been published in many journals, magazines and anthologies, he resides in the UK, from Manchester; he is the author of "In Perpetuity" and "Back on Earth" two books of poems published by a CTU publishing group, ~ Creative Talents Unleashed.

The Japanese Garden - Goran Petrovic

Only in a Japanese garden
Can you push all your worries aside,
Get rid of emotions ardent,
And find the stillness of your mind.

Close your eyes and withdraw
From this world full of passion and hate,
Listen to the birds chirping
On the beams of the Torii gate.

Hear them twitter their wisdom
of a humble and carefree life,
learn from the avian species
how to live without strife.

Then look at the carp in the creek,
Note how with ease it can swim,
Learn how to be swum by the current
'stead of swimming against the stream;

Learn how to keep your spirit
In a state of enduring bliss,
How, despite all distractions,
To maintain your mental peace.

Only in a Japanese garden
Can you leave all your worries behind,
Get rid of your passions ardent,
And find the stillness of your mind.

Goran Petrovic, PhD, is a Serbian humanities scholar dealing with British and American literature, especially utopian and SF literature. He is also a translator of literary works as well as scientific and technical texts. He writes rhyming poetry. So far, his work has appeared in Creativity Webzine.

Early April - Harriet Ribot

No more woodland scene
impressing us how casual time can be
draping a rotted limb
across a sapling tree
across a bough bursting with buds.

Interspersed between
layers of leaves anchored with moisture,
cocky empty cans peer,
blunted ends with blunted purpose
stopgap satisfaction on a road in time.

Discarded yellow plastic —
too bright for April's early promise —
tells of careless trespass.

No more woodland scene
speaking only of unhurried time
settling its way to the future
layering the past with leaves
showing a ribbon of time.

Harriet Ribot, age 94, has written for most of her life. At twenty she became an RN, served as an Emergency Room nurse, then worked with the American Red Cross. After raising four boys, she attended Rutgers University and completed her BA at age fifty-eight. She has only recently begun to share her work.

Creek Theory – Robert Okaji

Shaping itself, it absorbs.
Or accepts the path
of least resistance.
Without flesh, lacking
vertebrae, yet whole and sinuous,
writhing, capturing, releasing,
withholding, enabling, strewing.
It wants nothing, or wants only
those things we cannot know
or imagine. That bright
sorrow concealed in shale.
A collapsing star
in the heart of a catfish's
dream. Maybe the secrets
an elm branch murmurs as it
tumbles downstream.
I have watched snakes
swim against flood waters
till exhaustion carries them
away. I have seen mayflies
court just out of reach,
turtles accept its embrace.
What desires do we share,
which whimsies do we follow?
Water is a gathering of pulses,
a midnight shiver, a scattering, a
body. A constellation of kisses.
An acceptance we seek.
A resistance for which we are forgiven.

Robert Okaji is a half-Japanese Texan seeking work in Indiana. His poetry has appeared or is forthcoming in riverSedge, Tipton Poetry Review, Clade Song, MockingHeart Review, Vox Populi, Genuine Gold and elsewhere.

The Separation - Katy Santiff

I don't want to disconnect myself for
you from the magic of my inner world.
I want to imagine that when I plunge
my fingers into the soft Spring dirt, they
find themselves inside the skin of toadstools
and upon removing them again from
the earth, mushrooms emerge like the dewy
bulbs of an inverted glove. I want to
imagine that when I drag my fingers
out upon the night sky, space shimmers and
these stars ripple like light reflects disturbed
upon the darkest water. I want to
imagine that when the wind heaves through the
trees on a hot day, summer is breathing
heavy. I want to still imagine that
somewhere below us sugar lies in veins
like salt and the roots of honeysuckle
mine it. I want to imagine that when
I imagine so big that my senses
rush, this buzz is felt in shudders through the
world–and as long as somewhere in a glen
glossy bees are humming, I love you there.

Katy Santiff has written poetry in various forms all her life. A fan of meter and rhyme, she loves lines that hypnotize the reader with their sound. She believes in densely packed poems, preferring them to be a mouthful when read aloud. A lifelong Marylander, she loves waterside living.

On Thomas Doughty's *Landscape with Curving River* - Kelly Keener

The Lord hath dipped His brush
And painted upon organic earth.
The golden hues, His eminence bright,
Reflect in clouds near Heaven's height.

Marigold ink billows and froths
In echoes of the steady stream
Of yonder river among the glade,
Reflecting Autumn in quiet staid.

Antiquity nods her stately head
To dyes of crimson foliage,
And bids goodbye to dying limbs
Solemnly humming death's mournful hymns.

Yet, whilst death intercedes, subdued whispers
Hush the earth with pearl and ecru.
The Divine hand, Who fearfully inspires,
Hath moulded earth, the poet's lyre.

Kelly is a lover of 19th century American literature, and much of what she reads influences her work. When she isn't writing or transcribing under her pen name, Ann Neilson, for her blog, The Literary Maiden, she is hiding within the pages of works by Charles Fenno Hoffman, Henry William Herbert, and Elizabeth Oakes Smith.

In the End the Days - Joel Scarfe

The pond at the end of the road
was low and enclosed by trees
in a ring, a circling
of watchfulness
to bring a kind of judgement on our backs,
a sort of pre-emptive wreckage
on our newly folded boat
papering its maiden voyage
in a water
muddied to the visibility of inches.
In the end the days, each one
will unpeel its division
and become a single entity, unified
and luminescent

at the darkening edge of a lifetime.

Joel Scarfe's poems feature internationally in magazines, periodicals and anthologies including Black Lives Matter: Poems for a New World, and Brought to Sight and Swept Away. He lives in Bristol UK with the Danish ceramicist Rebecca Edelmann and their two children.

Conversation - Natalli Amato

There have been mornings
when I've seen water and sky as one
while I myself was in the same tender state:
Mind, soul, together.

It was those same mornings
when I heard the water speak
and held the sound
within me.

Today I went to the water,
hoping.

I could not become silent enough
to hear it.

Natalli Amato is the author of two poetry collections, "Burning Barrel" and "On a A Windless Night." She writes for Rolling Stone and Vice and is from Sackets Harbor, NY.

Winter Woods - Doug Bolling

Snow brings it.
Need to leave behind
Terrain of street and
Steel missiles rushing
On tires horns ablast.

The still untamed woods,
Uncertain extent, roads
Not yet paved as if to prove
Some misguided will to
Power.

Snow deepening as I walk,
The lights of town no match.
My tracks vanishing with
Each step I take,
A satisfying lostness.

Howl of north wind through
Fir and pine saying this is the
Real you left behind too many
Years ago, drive deeper
Deeper.

I stop to catch breath
surely watched by deer
And fox, true owners
Of this wilding still
Pristine, no sins allowed.

Nighttime nearing,
I could turn and flee,

Another surrender.
Better, I can choose to
Build warmth from

A fire's comforting
Resting here where
Snow and wind and
A mind's shifting balance
Make peace.

Doug Bolling's poetry has appeared in Water-Stone Review, Blueline, Basalt, Kestrel, Slant and previously in Vita Brevis among others. He has received Pushcart and Best of the Net Nominations and several awards and lives next door to Chicago.□

Pastoral – Shelley Saposnik

This wide space, this seemingly forward plain
on whose surface I've levied more lives than one.

In a little shack, perhaps one room and a room aside
I smell the rich soil, dark and fertile.
Here, where no concrete mars the wheat blowing
golden seeds through the air,
black and granite might as well be extinct.
Far from urban slogans and expensive shops
or the hidden heaviness of city air,
days are marked by the rise and fall of the sun.
Where once there was a slate of ice for a soul,
now there is wind blowing music, softly, easily through me
and to my right, a man's red hair pops out of covers.
He rolls over, wakes briefly to say:
To bed with you. Come now to bed, my love.
I return to thoughts under flickering candles.
Light and dark, gray shadows dancing
within and without, fragile, deep.
I live the day hot and round.
In the morning he will rise, that redhead there,
will stretch his arms and yawn.
Then out to the field with him and me.
Perhaps a poem is cooking, sizzling in the pan
with eggs and hash browns.

A day of work, an evening of music.
My lover sleeps, my lover sleeps.

Shelley Saposnik acquired a B.A. from Columbia University where she graduated with honors in English Literature, and an M.F.A. in Writing from Vermont College of Fine Arts. Currently, she teaches Modern European and Renaissance Literature at Touro College. Her most recent published poems appear in Sad Girls Literary Club, The Jewish Literary Journal and The Curator Magazine.

Cockatoos - Marilyn Humbert

We hear rasping squawks
above the eucalypt canopy
the hour before twilight, clamour
riffles air currents and leaf-tassels.

First one bird floats down, then two and more
a flock of white-winged clouds,
a host of raucous angels
land beside the muddy river.

A crackle of yellow crested cockatoos
catch the last rays of sun between reed swathes,
dancing bob-style, preen and sip,
gargle in the shallows.

Under-age larrikins swagger,
chatter like school-kids on excursion,
onyx-eyes sharp, watchful, as sunset pink overlays
the day's blue beside the Murray.

Each evening we watch their display
wondering why the flock returns
to the same sandy shingle.
An imprint passed from matriarch to egg.
A ritual learnt in the nest.

Then whoosh, the cohort takes flight
braids and folds, circles the gathering gloom
to roost on high branches, their goodnights
fall silent as the day moon brightens.

Just you and me, the slow swirl of water
among the edge reeds.

Marilyn Humbert lives in the Northern suburbs of Sydney NSW Australia. Her tanka and haiku appear in international and Australian journals, anthologies and online. Her free verse poems have been awarded prizes in competitions and some have been published most recently in The Burrow and Poetry for the Planet.

The Sound of Rain - Megha Sood

The sound of rain needs no translation
It's pure and serene,
as it impinges upon the earth
like your fleeting touch on my skin

The pitter-patter of drops
that symphony,
which breeds through nature's and takes you in
every drop holds a universe,
a plethora of memories to bask in

I can get drenched by every falling drop
till the skies cry to their heart's content
as it falls relentlessly on my skin and washes every sin

This ambrosial experience
this seraphic touch,
A gift from the skies to the earth with its parched skin

Sounds of rain need no translation
as it slowly seeps in.

Megha Sood is an Award-Winning Poet, Editor, Author, based in New Jersey, USA. Associate Editor at MookyChick(UK), Life and Legends (USA), and Literary Partner "Life in Quarantine" with Stanford University, USA. Chapbook ("My Body is Not an Apology", Finishing Line Press, 2021) and Full Length ("My Body Lives Like a Threat", FlowerSongPress,2021).

Bus Ride - Kathryn Sadakierski

Deer grazed
Under gardens of skycolor,
Sunrise paint,
Unknown to any manufacturers.
Further down the road a ways,
Later in the day,
You'd see horses
Happily in their blankets,
Fenced in by mountains,
Pastures,
And sunset.

The mountains were not mired
In shadow, with faces inscrutable,
But smiled contentedly,
With upturned faces,
When the nascent rays of sun
Smoothed their foreheads,
And they were like children
Prancing in and out of the waves,
Laughing at the beach,
Warmed by the sand,
Inner comfort,
Natural born joy,
In a cocoon of light,

Stirred by mountains gold
As the autumn harvest,
Nuggets of corn,
Baptized by a veil of pink,
Light as strawberry frosting,
Liquid soft, as melted chocolate,

In a thin sheen of frost,
Flecks that shimmered
As fish scales do,
In undulating trains that light skips across,
Playing hopscotch,
Fingers trotting down piano keys,
(Strolling down the street),
Continuous cords,
All folded in with the batter of gold.

The dairy cows were lined at their stalls,
Mosaics of black and white,
Assemblies breakfasting,
Unfazed, tails swishing
Like reeds bobbing along a river
Moving at its leisure.
By afternoon, the heady odor
Of cow patties
Would seep in through
The shaky, smudged windows
On the high school bus
That never seemed to shut.

For now, the morning was clean,
Anything could be,
And I anxiously sat in my seat,
Orisons maneuvering
Through my brain
(Like gleaners among rows of crops,
Harvesting,
Mining through the gold),
Painted in with the mountains,
That John Deere mailbox, a landmark,

Barns, rusty tractors,
Open fields like unraveled fabric,
Sewing patterns.

Though I passed this way each day,
All the sunrises new,
Streaming into the next,
I ached for poetry then,
Not knowing that it was
Everywhere, all around me,
In the verses of the mountains,
Gold and pink,
More vivid than memory;
My heart recites these odes each day,
Remembered, felt, beauty,
Impressed like flowers in my soul.

Kathryn Sadakierski's writing has appeared in Critical Read, Halfway Down the Stairs, Literature Today, NewPages Blog, Northern New England Review, and elsewhere. Her micro-chapbook "Travels through New York" was published by Origami Poems Project (2020). She graduated summa cum laude with a B.A. and M.S. from Bay Path University.

The Cedar Tree - Lucia Coppola

There are several stories in this story. This is typical of cedars.
The roots tell of branches which tell of shadows, which tell of light
and magic and seasons and ordinary people passing, telling stories
of the story telling cedar tree, as I do now with this one in France.

There was once a grand vizier who came from the east with a gift
opulent and sensual, scented, oriental, ornate and fundamental as gold,
frankincense, myrrh - a grand and little thing to make a stir.
What else would one give to a king?

But it really began with a botanist - Bernard de Jussieu
who wore them in his hat one day after stumbling and breaking pots
on his way to a ceremonious reverence to the king with pirouette,
alouette, gentille lark whistling a winsome tune to sun and moon

and back again as not long after more cedar trees would grow, planted
by a woman for her husband, the floral painter Redouté, one tree each day
as children were born with roots and branches knitting the years and yawning
this diddy of the painter, the woman, the cedars growing and the city

where gentlefolk and merry pranksters still poke round here now with talk
that travels back to Jerusalem, the temple, Noah, the ark, paper scrolls
made of bark, before we could read or had heard anyone say a word
about the wheel, the worship of idols, pots and pans, the uses of clay

Gilgamesh - in cuneiform script on tablets, sword in hand roams the land,
combats shadow, light, frost, twists, turns, and snow before
he penetrates the forest door of Ishtar, Mother of the Kish, Uruk, Ur -
realizing anyone can die from a snakebite - the poison or simply the wound

anyone - though we can now count to ten, make digital prints of back then
and me, for example, here on the branch of this mighty tree, watching
children explore the contours and height, languishing as I do in the dappled
late afternoon light. This too is worth recounting.

As an old French dictum says:
"The greater the tree, the greater its shadow."
This alone tells ...
quite a lot.

Lucia Coppola is an ESL teacher who is originally from New York and has lived in France since 1985. She has a professional background in dance and body techniques. Her writing is largely informed by nature, traditional storytelling and by where she lives near the forest of Paris. Some of her work has been read on the New River Clocktower Radio program in New York City and published with Inspirelle, The Parliament Literary Magazine and the Plants and Poetry Anthology.

Undertow - Shelley Saposnik

I run toward a breaking wave and crash into its underbelly

pressing me down and down and down
through layers of sea green and memory.
There are the woods where I am lost,
where salamanders hang around with frogs.
There is the little blond girl I wanted to be, me –
dark haired and brown-skinned from the rays
of a Rockaway sun.
See? There is my brother. Pale and ghostly.
I want to grab him before he's gone from me
forever. My brother whom I cannot save.
Down and down and down into the colors of the sea,
waves of dark and indigo and copper
reflections from above –the mirrored life the water gives up
days—when ecstasy was a right you had, easy.
My God it's all there.
And the shimmering, enveloping quiet piercing your soul
as deeper you go, tells of who you are, were
and will become.

I soar to the surface, and gulp the fresh, salted air.

Shelley Saposnik acquired a B.A. from Columbia University where she graduated with honors in English Literature, and an M.F.A. in Writing from Vermont College of Fine Arts. Currently, she teaches Modern European and Renaissance Literature at Touro College. Her most recent published poems appear in Sad Girls Literary Club, The Jewish Literary Journal and The Curator Magazine.

Prayer to Autumn - Mary Wynne

Speak to me
In the ripples of your bronzed pond
Let your silent waves
Take my incessant thoughts
Beneath the surface
Where there is no sound

I want to feel you
Inside of me
Telling me it's time to let go
To sink to the bottom
And join your fallen children
Those colored leaves
Who can give no more

Let me lay upon your breast
Engorged with decay
And drink
Until my empty veins are full
And all memory of desire
Slips away

I pray I will grow within you
Laying roots
Sprouting stems
Bearing new leaves
Until I can speak in silent waves
Calling all lost souls to listen
And let go

Mary Wynne studied English literature at the University of Minnesota a million years ago, the same time she also published her first poem. After a few decades of growing children and a career to support those children, she has returned to her love of reading and writing poetry. Her poem "The Long Night" was selected by Vita Brevis Press for the anthology Brought to Sight & Swept Away. Her work has also been featured on Spillwords and Uppagus. She has completed two self-published chapbooks, Reconciliation and Hindsight. She is currently thinking about what to do next.

Home - Cynthia Pitman

When they ask where I am,
tell them I went kayaking –
meandered downriver
seeking the hidden cove
arched with water oaks
dripping their gray Spanish moss.
Tell them I'll stay there,
eyes closed, mind clear,
in the cool air of this leafy cavern
until dark. Not until then
will I make my way back,
only to go back again and again
to find the roots of where I began.

Cynthia Pitman has been published in Vita Brevis, Pain and Renewal, Brought to Sight & Swept Away, Amethyst Review, Ekphrastic Journal, Third Wednesday (One Sentence Poem finalist), Saw Palm (Pushcart Prize nominee), Red Fez (Story of the Week), and others. Her book, The White Room, was published in 2020 by Kelsay Books.

Irene 2 - Katy Santiff

You weren't prepared for this at all: the glance
and graze, love pooling up from old cellars
that flood like spring thaws out the ribboned
ice within their walls — welling dampness of
this draw — scents of darkness/earth that paw
at you, at memories of me finding things
that fall within the woods, branches not built
for suckling sap from trunks and went down when
the weight of some small bird pressed down, unheard.
No, you weren't ready for that snap, and then
descent towards independence — and when
the ground surrounded you, when leaves laid out
their crinkled capes before and floored you —
you were not ready for the forest yet.
You were meant to be a sky thing, don't forget.

Katy Santiff has written poetry in various forms all her life. A fan of meter and rhyme, she loves lines that hypnotize the reader with their sound. She believes in densely packed poems, preferring them to be a mouthful when read aloud. A lifelong Marylander, she loves waterside living.

The Turning of the Leaves - Erina Booker

I have answered
with Spring
time and again,
the swell of sap
in green gestation
a profusion of bloom

and then
like a time-lapse image
I have answered
also
with conflagrations
of colour:
fiery pyres
of scarlet, maroon, cerise,
and the unexpected
peach

now it's time for peace –
my years clustered like snow,
my hair
fragrant
from leaf smoke,
ashy
from burned bridges.

Erina Booker is a Sydney-based poet. Her life revolves around poetry, from publishing books and contributing to journals, to recitals at public events and presentation of seminars. She actively supports poetry in her local community. Erina holds a B.A. in Literature and Composition, and a Graduate Degree in Counselling. She knows the value of words and the pauses between them.

The Swamp Oak - Ed Ahern

Balding leafage
lets the eye slip through
to scabrous bark
that runs past rot holes
hiding squirrels.

Twisted branches
contort around power lines,
reaching upward
and straining to
recover grace.

The tree sways
toward a century
it will not reach,
and strews its seeds
with wanton hope.

Ed Ahern resumed writing after forty odd years in foreign intelligence and international sales. He's had over three hundred stories and poems published so far, and six books. Ed works the other side of writing at Bewildering Stories, where he sits on the review board and manages a posse of nine review editors.

Scape - Jane Blanchard

(Previously published in The Kerf)

For years each bulb put forth one daffodil —
A yellow trumpet of the winter's end.
The energetic blooms were welcome till
I noticed fewer blowing. As the trend
Continued, I endeavored to pretend
Each February an anomaly.
Not so, of course. Although the bulbs did send
New shoots through warming soil, their potency
Was waning, slowly, surely. Two or three
Inch-thin green leaves was what most could produce
At this late stage. I knew eventually
None would be capable of springing juice.
I dug up every bulb my shovel found,
Let pines deliver needles to the ground.

Jane Blanchard lives and writes in Georgia (USA). Her poetry has recently been published in Australia, Austria, Canada, Israel, the Netherlands, the United Kingdom, and the United States. Her latest collection is Never Enough Already (2021).

Ancient Land - Marilyn Humbert

Capertee Valley air is still.
Insects rise and scatter as we walk
sun-struck sandstone escarpments.
Hazy eucalypts draw eyes to the summit.

Boots grip roots uncovered by erosion.
Native bees hover, settling on a patch of yellow
fill the gap between us. I stumble
against a casuarina's rough bark

scrambling the slope, lagging behind
to watch brown jenny wrens bob
between stalks, electric-blue males
tail feathers flicking, ignore our intrusion.

From an outcrop halfway to the crest
the valley lies flat, exposed. A sinuous river
carves pasture and forest. It's here we stop
ancient land warm beneath our soles.

Your steadying hand enfolds mine.
We leave no trace in passing.

Marilyn Humbert lives in the Northern suburbs of Sydney NSW Australia. Her tanka and haiku appear in international and Australian journals, anthologies and online. Her free verse poems have been awarded prizes in competitions and some have been published most recently in The Burrow and Poetry for the Planet.

Wishes – Jaya Avendel

Young leaves rustle. They were born yesterday.
Dappled shade cleanses my face.

I hold the damp earth in my palm and
Massage it into my skin. Hands to the ground I uncover a
Twisted glass soda bottle from 1926.
Whistle: orange fizzy drink. Cap still on.

The base is broken
Twin glass shards fall onto the earth
This genie did not wait to be set free.

Jaya Avendel is a word witch from the Blue Ridge Mountains of Virginia, passionate about life where it intersects with writing and the dreamscapes lost in between. She shares writing tips, publication news, and further poetry at "ninchronicles.com."

Near the End of Ocean Boulevard
- Jane Blanchard

(Previously runner-up in the Robert Frost Poetry Contest)

The county's latest bulwark has begun
to fail already—maybe only weeks
since normal traffic was allowed back on
this busy stretch of road. Saltwater seeps,
then undermines concrete too easily.
No engineer has figured out a way
to stop erosion here. Predictably
tides entering and leaving every day
will do their damage. Nature takes care of
its own—the egrets, herons, ibises,
wood storks, and clapper rails which perch above
or nest in marsh grass after meals. What is
a human being in this habitat?
A passerby who gets a glance, if that.

Jane Blanchard lives and writes in Georgia (USA). Her poetry has recently been published in Australia, Austria, Canada, Israel, the Netherlands, the United Kingdom, and the United States. Her latest collection is Never Enough Already (2021).

The Oak Tree - Lucia Coppola

Not the truth - just a lens - a spectrum of possibilities
amidst the rollicking leaves when going there along
what looks like a trail, though we usually just amble
through shafts and flickers of light toward the oak
which is as close as we ever get to a destination
with no indication but the veil of sunlight, fog or rain
shared with a friend - a tree, a rock, a stump in the sun
for a brief stop in winter and with the fall of night

Not the way - just a feeling - a mood that hovers like a film and
alters color depending on how we do the trip - bicycles
no cars or motorcycles, no virtual screens. The simplest way
is on foot - a transfer of weight and an inclination forwards

And a point of view amongst pine cones and leaves
and treasures that exult in their own serendipity
like the big white heart we found painted on a tree trunk
when we had just been talking about love
And cleaning up litter on the way - a chance
to bring some air to the earth as we clear the ground for a crow
to land and stare cross-eyed at us saying whatever crows say

And the thrill of reading signs, avoiding holes and bramble
that creep up unforeseen and badger about uncertainty, survival,
being upside down and picking nettles out of hair - the relief
of getting past parasites, the scorn of others, prowlers at night

Not a religion - Just a tree - a companion we look in on,
an elder of the community and witness to our words - a tree
that filters the daily din and bids us to come and curl up
to breathe, to lean steadfast into day with a sense of destination,
with roots like arms that extend all around so we want to linger
and travel back again to where

a squirrel passes, acorns stuffed into its little cheeks, an owl hoots
with the fall of the night - a crow lands with urgency and says...
How do you spell it? C-A-W - Yes, double U
one U that journeys and one U that stays
One U that stays right here by the oak

Lucia Coppola is an ESL teacher who is originally from New York and has lived in France since 1985. She has a professional background in dance and body techniques. Her writing is largely informed by nature, traditional storytelling and by where she lives near the forest of Paris. Some of her work has been read on the New River Clocktower Radio program in New York City and published with Inspirelle, The Parliament Literary Magazine and the Plants and Poetry Anthology.

Hillside Trees - Ed Ahern

There are just a few days for hillside trees,
when each tree's special shade
shimmers through fresh spring rain
and proclaims itself unique;
and again when thick summer sap
thins enough to bare the pale jades,
brief intervals when their voices are heard,
not in Grand Forest chorus, but in haunting arias
that end perfectly and too soon.

Ed Ahern resumed writing after forty odd years in foreign intelligence and international sales. He's had over three hundred stories and poems published so far, and six books. Ed works the other side of writing at Bewildering Stories, where he sits on the review board and manages a posse of nine review editors.

A Variety of One Thing - Harriet Ribot

I don't mind the rain,
it limits where I want to run—
makes my day more manageable,

cushions the strident
street sounds
and channels my thinking

into rivulets
of vertical run-off
and up again,

beating out different rhythms
of varying intensity
and patterns

against my windshield,
my eyeglasses,
my world. Here,

I see the pointillism of a Seurat
temporally
sown by nature.

There, a shadowy
Monet figure, moving,
escaping its frame.

How seldom we are
completely absorbed
by a variety of one thing

—like an autistic child

into whose world
few can intrude.

Doctors say
if you threaten
a schizophrenic's system of beliefs

they might 'act-out' their
bizarre thoughts. Into what
would I translate

my fascination
with raindrops, with a rainstorm
— if interrupted?

Would I be taken away from the world?
No — for I have long practiced
breaking connections.

I have learned to disconnect
myself and resettle
a fragment of me on paper.

Harriet Ribot, age 94, has written for most of her life. At twenty she became an RN, served as an Emergency Room nurse, then worked with the American Red Cross. After raising four boys, she attended Rutgers University and completed her BA at age fifty-eight. She has only recently begun to share her work.

I am Immersed in a River
- Lynda McKinney Lambert

I am immersed in a river that
flows in every season.
I rest in the shade of
hemlocks and ferns
gather water-worn stones from
the whirling floor of a cool eddy.
In my red canoe I skim the surface of
the emerald-green mountain river
while russet and gold autumn trees
prepare for winter's respite.

Lynda, a retired professor of fine arts and humanities, Geneva College in Pennsylvania, authored 5 published books that focus on spare poems and thoughtful personal essays. Lynda lives with her husband Bob, their 2 dogs and 6 cats. Lynda's love of nature, fine art, and history provide her dominate themes.

Homing – Jaya Avendel

In imaging myself an urban girl
With snake tongue and philodendron for trees
The evening city a descent of stars
A piece of myself
The woman with walnut-stained hair
Who transplanted an ancient rhubarb plant
From one crumbling mountain home to hers
Whispers free.

I let her grow
She is a firefly who always returns to her woods.

Jaya Avendel is a word witch from the Blue Ridge Mountains of Virginia, passionate about life where it intersects with writing and the dreamscapes lost in between. She shares writing tips, publication news, and further poetry at "ninchronicles.com."

Search for the 'Lord God Bird' - Carolyn Martin

-Scrubgrass Bayou, Arkansas

Naturalists are slogging through
these swampy bottomlands to find
a feathered-black, white-lightning backed,
red-crested bird supposedly extinct.
For sixty years this Picidae
has cheated death – or so they think.

Population? One's a probable,
says Audubon, at most a few;
but this is breeding time and that takes two.

So Ivory-billed woodpecker teams
fight catclaw briars, locust thorns,
and whiplash vines that slow the time
they race against to catch the two-foot wings.
They still insist this bird exists
and needs recovery.

But bayous aren't level playing fields.
This bird's outsmarted satellites
and infrareds with flash strobe lights
and copters flying low to flush it out.
High instinct always trumps high tech
when privacy's in doubt.

Though I'm no ornithologist,
I fantasize that in the marshy deeps
the Lord of tree death and decay,
the God of ancient forest ruins, appraises
his domain. From his catbird seat, he re-assures
his mate, *No headline-making finds today.*

(Previously published in VoiceCatcher4)

Carolyn Martin is a lover of gardening, feral cats, backyard birds, writing, and photography. Her poems have appeared in more than 135 journals throughout North America, Australia, and the UK. She is the poetry editor of Kosmos Quarterly: journal for global transformation.

Morning, Berkshires - John Muro

This day tests the value
Of vision; all distance
Measured by ear; the
Emerging particulars
Of acorns, in hushed
Hurl, slapping the under-
Side of leaves and plucking
Ground; of lake waters
Lapping in muffled slush
Beneath a ridge line half-
Hidden in mists. Where a
Catbird's cry, fraught with
Anguish, moves against me
And gives voice to a fore-
Boding that settles uneasily
After an evening interspersed
With rain. Then this strange
And shapeless silence and
An emptiness that seems
Unfathomable – feeling
More than a day's dying
And wondering what it is
That we are married to, what
Has changed and what, more
Precisely, has been taken from us?

A resident of Connecticut, John's first volume of poems, In the Lilac Hour, was published last fall by Antrim House, and it is available on Amazon. His poems have been published or are forthcoming in numerous literary journals, including River Heron, Moria, Sheepshead, Euphony, Writer Shed and the French Literary Review. John is a two-time Pushcart Prize nominee.

The Winter Day is Steadily Declining
- Kelly Keener

The Winter day is steadily declining,
and a hushed, blanketed mist gently descends
upon thatched roofs, languidly spreading
its dreary web o'er the wearisome heads
returning from hard day's labour.
A forgiving hearth reconciles debt and dismay,
and beckons, with sensuous snapping, to stay.
Ice-crystal branches peck and prod, and beg, too,
to escape the chill, whilst sharp winds blowing,
moaning, warn of the oncoming storm.
The house settles, the fire dims,
and an unsolicited chill crawls down our lungs,
extinguishing warmth, enwrapping our bones,
callously coating with hoary frost—
A log is placed, the fire's ablaze,
and unbidden thoughts are ceased,
cast to the wind,
and warmth perpetuates the soul once more.

Kelly is a lover of 19th century American literature, and much of what she reads influences her work. When she isn't writing or transcribing under her pen name, Ann Neilson, for her blog, The Literary Maiden, she is hiding within the pages of works by Charles Fenno Hoffman, Henry William Herbert, and Elizabeth Oakes Smith.

Barn Owl - Christian Ward

No barn owls in central London,
so why is there one perched
above my wardrobe? Crouched
like an old man to avoid the ceiling,
it peers with binocular sight
at my attempt to describe its heart-like
face round as an apple slice. Too
much? The bird says nothing
when my fingers press on, aiming
for *Elizabethan* for a tuft of feathers.
I wait for its call. Only silence. I wait
again for a call, some validation
heavy as its flight, heavy as prey
in its talons. The owl is silent like myself
in mass. Should I continue? Add
a detail like *its beak is a compass needle?*
Only the silence white as its chest.
Its feathers have born the brunt
of autumn, cannot be shed by the quiverful.
I pause before thinking of the silence
of masses, how I am a priest in my own
church that changes from field to cathedral
to field, its contents laid out like unidentified pellets.

Christian Ward is a UK-based writer who can be currently found in Wild Greens, Cold Moon Journal, Discretionary Love, Chantarelle's Notebook and Medusa's Kitchen. Future poems will be appearing in Dreich, Uppagus, Impspired and Spry. □

These Appalachians – John Grey

They were much higher once
but tune has worn the Appalachians down.

Those days of thrusting upward
were like young adulthood,
believing that ridgelines
just grow higher and higher
and no sky is safe.

But, for old peaks and ranges,
everything's rounded off
like a paycheck
to the penny below,
shapes are smoothed,
rocks are broken like a colt.

From, now on,
these mountains
will be amiable and forested,
safe and satisfied with morning mist,
seasonal change,
flush with wildlife
while providing instruction in nature
to the occasional hiker.

The Appalachians no longer soar
but they have found an acceptable level.
A hawk peers down from a fluttering pine-top.
A black bear nibbles on berry-laden bushes.
The mountains are just low enough
so they can get away with this.

John Grey is an Australian poet, US resident, recently published in Sheepshead Review, Poetry Salzburg Review and Hollins Critic. Latest books, "Leaves On Pages" and "Memory Outside The Head" are available through Amazon. Work upcoming in Lana Turner and International Poetry Review.

The Reality of Aging - Charles Portolano

When I was ten, I wandered alone
deeper into the woods, finding
a clearing where a massive red oak
stood at the far edge of the forest,
towering above all the other trees,
standing guard over the entrance
of the wonderous, magical forest.
I climbed to the top of this oak
and felt free high up in the sky,
with the wind blowing me around,
then happily dangling upside down
from one of the thick branches
feeling like a daredevil.
I learned that day if I held still,
silenced my thoughts, I could hear
all the creatures living in this tree,
everyday inching towards the heavens.

Each season I returned to witness
the leaves growing from bud,
to green, then to a rich red, and
finally, to fall to the forest floor.
I watched the deer and their fawns
devour the acorns on the ground;
watched the zany squirrels dart
crazily hunting for the nuts.
Over the years, I had many picnics
under the shade this tree provided.
Lost a girlfriend or two for refusing
to carve our initials into its bark.
I think of all its daily good deeds:
taking our CO_2, while giving oxygen;
giving hikers shelter from the storms.

And, oh, how many times have I hid
in its branches when the worries
of this cruel world surrounded me,
when the adults wouldn't listen to me,
but this oak listened without judgment,
never heard a harsh word from this tree,
everyday inching towards the heavens.

50 years have passed, I stand before this
oak tree, who has been a mentor to me,
saddened to see that a lightning bolt
struck it down, split it into two;
sad since it was in the autumn of its life.
It strikes me now how we can never know
when suddenly we could be struck down,
out of the blue to fall to the ground, gone.
Have I been inching towards the heavens?

Charles Portolano has been writing poetry for 26 years since the birth of his daughter, Valerie. He is the Editor/Publisher of The Avocet, a Journal of Nature Poetry. Since becoming editor, he only writes about Nature themes, especially those poems that reflect how we are losing our only home.

White Tail - John Muro

I've come unbidden to where pasture
Stumbles over an outcropping of low-
Lying stones and falls into mists that
Drift in and out of woodlands and
Deeper pockets of undergrowth and
Am taken by the lack of fear in her
Grazing, eyes near slumber and a
Loose garland of grasses dripping
From her mouth, as if she knows
That I, yet another of the bipedal tribe,
Am but a stray that life has softened
And parted from pain, senses dulled
By comfort, unfamiliar with the
Perpetual pangs of leaf-dappled fear
Where she waits upon fate and a twig
Snap could mean the difference between
The near- or far-side of death; nor,
Until that day, had I taken in the silent
Spectacle of flight, as she cleared the
Mottled stone wall with the ease of wind,
White tail lifted like a dismissive,
Gloved hand, slipping as softly as prayer
Thru the pleated curtains of leaves.

A resident of Connecticut, John's first volume of poems, In the Lilac Hour, was published last fall by Antrim House, and it is available on Amazon. His poems have been published or are forthcoming in numerous literary journals, including River Heron, Moria, Sheepshead, Euphony, Writer Shed and the French Literary Review. John is also a recent Pushcart Prize nominee.

Autumnal Prelude - Lynda McKinney Lambert

My sleek black cat stretches forward
views rain-soaked world through open window
sits quietly as early morning rain dribbles
soft metallic tunes on rainspouts
listens to chipmunks chattering
in rock-pile of my spare Japanese garden.

I listen as cars splash down flooded road
crows call from beyond the dense woods
deep olive-green dimness of tangled
swagging bittersweet vines
careening from highest maple trees

Rain alters my gardening schedules
tulip, crocus, and daffodil bulbs
remain unnoticed, dry and safe
after swift flight from Holland
the promise of a colorful spring garden
remains intact
resting in cardboard shipping box.

Autumnal days grow cooler
but soil remains warm
plants now focus their energy
on root development
preparing for their Spring performance.

Patience is a virtue for cats,
gardeners and plants.

Lynda, a retired professor of fine arts and humanities, Geneva College in Pennsylvania, authored 5 published books that focus on spare poems and thoughtful personal essays. Lynda lives with her husband Bob, their 2 dogs and 6 cats. Lynda's love of nature, fine art, and history provide her dominate themes.

Lichen - Christian Ward

Lichen on the neighbouring
roof an unknown language;
each yellow splatter a letter
of its undiscovered alphabet.

My hands can understand
the Braille of the roofing tiles
it has colonised, but the dandelion
shaped fractals of its symbols

are alien to me. Perhaps if I bleed
Morse it will unravel its message;
perhaps if I give it a curl of hair,
a fleck of skin, it will understand
a reply intricate and beautiful as a star.

*Christian Ward is a UK-based writer who can be currently found in Wild
Greens, Cold Moon Journal, Discretionary Love, Chantarelle's Notebook and
Medusa's Kitchen. Future poems will be appearing in Dreich, Uppagus,
Impspired and Spry.* □

Kaimana - Josie Rozell

With fistfuls of ocean, I scrub
the soles of my feet —
exhausting flakes for the fish food
watching the waves lose pieces
in a fist fight with the breeze.
I got a whole lotta sand
to figure things out.
The sun will wait for me
patiently kissing umbrella clouds
til my blue towel be set near that low wall.
Not for the first time do I wonder
how long this will last.
    Harnessing light from underneath garage doors
        I slide myself gently into the sea.

Josie Rozell is a Hawai'i-based indie poet and essayist. She is the author of Articulated Soul, a collection of poems and collage from five areas of the world, and is at work on her second book of poetry, Deep Breath, featuring sonnets and surrealist collage.□

Egret - John Grey

A fluffy white egret emerges
from the cattails,
wings pressed to its side
as it scours the edges of the pond.

While other birds soar,
the egret could live its life
between wind and air,
dark and light,
a slight disturbance in the muddy bottom
and a violent spearing.

Its slow steps
follow ancient guidelines.
Its eyes and ears,
even its talons,
are all sight.

John Grey is an Australian poet, US resident, recently published in Sheepshead Review, Poetry Salzburg Review and Hollins Critic. Latest books, "Leaves On Pages" and "Memory Outside The Head" are available through Amazon. Work upcoming in Lana Turner and International Poetry Review.

Future Grazing – Timothy Dodd

The Angus are on the run,
lifting their claws in slope
and sway, following hillside
relief of our flat-earth days.

Greater blue mountains look
down at them from a distance,
her bright red wineberry kiss
on edges of old pastureland.

With a black shine trickling
across the green, the stream
in their muscle, they bound
in their own moment of color.

But I think, one day the cattle
will catch our cars, may even
stop at the general store, butt
in — clean up what's left of us.

Timothy Dodd is from Mink Shoals, WV, and the author of Fissures, and Other Stories (Bottom Dog Press). His second collection of stories, Men in Midnight Bloom, is forthcoming (Cowboy Jamboree Press) as is a collection of poetry, Modern Ancient (High Window Press). Find a bit more writing on his 'Timothy Dodd, Writer' Facebook page.

Hundred Year Floodplain - Merridawn Duckler

The river rose and rose, the banks
blank as the water line crept
up where it had never been wet,
surpassed and spread in dark pools
or rain bowed from oils light
and sunk. Our dreams were wringing,
our thoughts like the wipers back and forth
back and forth, criers hidden, the mark
of the sky on all the clothes and lashes.
And still the water rose, terribly steady
under the sand bags and we woke to rivulets
gush in the streets, spread like fingers,
pouring on either side of a fist. The birds
shuffled among the puddles, unsure where to fly
and we shaded our eyes to watch them rise
into the white flat cloud cover through a slit
returning black from nowhere, flat as a cross.

Merridawn Duckler is a writer from Oregon, author of INTERSTATE (dancing girl press) and IDIOM (Washburn Prize, Harbor Review.) Winner of the 2021 Beullah Rose Poetry Contest. She's an editor at Narrative and the philosophy journal Evental Aesthetics.

Doves - Zara Raab

This is how you live when you're exposed and split.
As am I: twigs and a bit of moss or lint
tucked in at the elbow of the sumac.
With my small heart, I am almost weightless.
Something stirs in the needle of my compass.
Hour by hour, weathers unsettle and pass
from clear light swept in from the Atlantic
to wind currents twisting through the dusk,
menace to the small button flowers late-
blooming in the too-green, wet-summer grass.

Penned beneath this dome of sky, we flit,
alert to topographies of coming snow.
We'll carry word to the others. For now,
you know as well as I to watch and wait,
know what will be is always uncertain.
Clouds mass, a sudden downpour. Split again,
the wind dies down, the sumac leaves drip rain,
silky fisher-martins after squirrel run
by the stone wall at the field's sloping end
that any year a rising sea may flood.

(Previously published in Think: A Journal of Poetry, Fiction and Essays)

*Zara Raab will release two of her books, Swimming the Eel and Fracas &
Asylum, in a combined New Edition later this year. Her work, including book
reviews, as well as poems, has appeared in The Hudson Review, Verse Daily,
River Styx, West Branch, Arts & Letters, Critical Flame, Prime Number, Raven
Chronicles, and The Dark Horse. She recently joined the Powow River Poets
north of Boston.*

Ghyllside - Craig Dobson

What if he was the glory of foxes –
snout pointing to the Pole star,
his belly whitening the winter dusk,
his stillness by the water, lying?
Caught in his stride, his brush
still touching the nettled edge
he passed through in the night –
as if this place had caught him
in a promise of more than all
his senses, held him in a snare
of moonlight, and laid him quiet
on his side, here among shadows
and ice on this, the shortest day.

Craig's been published in Acumen, Agenda, Butcher's Dog, Crannóg, The Dark Horse, Ink, Sweat and Tears, The Interpreter's House, The Literary Hatchet, The London Magazine, Magma, Neon, New Welsh Review, The North, Poetry Ireland Review, Poetry Salzburg Review, Prole, The Rialto, Stand, Southword, THINK, Under The Radar and Vita Brevis.

That Yeats Thing - Craig Dobson

Beneath a ridge of mist-torn raven calls,
where a forlorn ruin's lease
haunts its tumbled dry stone walls
and the lapping shore's deserted peace,

I hear only diesels cough and bus brakes wracking,
the fury of car horns waning sirens down
to a monotonous prophecy of trains stacking
crowded stares on the phone-loud town

at whose tarmac core – its reflection worn thin
by endless flights crawling
their noise over its shoreless skin –
a park pond worries the litter on its heartsick calling.

Craig's been published in Acumen, Agenda, Butcher's Dog, Crannóg, The Dark Horse, Ink, Sweat and Tears, The Interpreter's House, The Literary Hatchet, The London Magazine, Magma, Neon, New Welsh Review, The North, Poetry Ireland Review, Poetry Salzburg Review, Prole, The Rialto, Stand, Southword, THINK, Under The Radar and Vita Brevis.

Nocturnal Orchestrations - Michele Mekel

Twilight gathers,
as winds whisper through standing talls,
their rustling leaves sharing secrets of nightfall.
Caressed by evening breeze,
Shekinah's waters lap softly against her banks,
murmuring gentle melodies.
A chorus of frogs calls and responds,
exchanging raspy harmonies,
until dawn breaches the eastern horizon.
And midnight's sentinels, enrobed in fur and feathers,
cry appeals to Grandmother Moon,
punctuating the never-silent night.

Michele Mekel wears many hats: bioethicist, educator, poetess, cat herder, and woman. Her work appears in academic and creative publications, and has been featured on Garrison Keillor's The Writer's Almanac, nominated for Best of the Net, and translated into Cherokee. She is co-principal investigator of Viral Imaginations: COVID-19 (viralimaginations.psu.edu).

Covenant - Ron. Lavalette

There is nothing ambiguous about
the absence of sunshine this morning;
nothing open to interpretation; nothing
equivocal. No. This morning
on the lawn—if brown can be a lawn,
if a lawn can be a mat of last year's leaves—
this morning's lawn, then, is frost alone,
no new snow anywhere, just cold
and a frosty glaze, the promise
of impending winter.

Ron. Lavalette lives on Vermont's Canadian border. His poetry, flash fiction, and creative nonfiction has been very widely published in both print and pixel forms. His first chapbook, Fallen Away (Finishing Line Press), is now available at all standard outlets. A reasonable sample of his work can be found at EGGS OVER TOKYO.

Watching the Lake - Carol Grametbauer

The mallards glide toward shore
like a trio of small skiffs, sprout legs
at water's edge, and clamber
up the rocky bank, pick at snails
in the weeds, then turn in unison
and gaze across the rippled water
where they'd been. Tranquility

blankets a late-June afternoon:
sunlight on leaves, cicadas' grind,
soft chuff of waves from a passing
pontoon boat. On the dock,
a great blue heron, motionless
as if crafted from pewter;
in the air, swarms of mayflies
frantic to procreate before the sun
goes down. We watch together, heron,
ducks, and I — the clouds of insects,
water's gentle roll toward the shore.

Watch: the lake unchanging, the lake
ever-changing. At length the mallards slide
again into its aquamarine light, the heron
hoists its broad gray wings and flies.
I stay behind, and watch the lake.

Carol Grametbauer is the author of two chapbooks: *Homeplace* (Main Street Rag, 2018), and *Now & Then* (Finishing Line Press, 2014). Her poems have appeared in numerous journals including *Appalachian Heritage, Connecticut River Review, Pine Mountain Sand & Gravel*, and *The Sow's Ear Poetry Review*, and in several anthologies.

Mingled - Leah M. Hill

Fog mingled among the trees,
Whispering, giggling –
Entwining branches,
Brushing its fingertips against leafy veins.
I watched it parade its temporary glory,
Fleeting, fading when light pierced its robe.
Raging through the trees,
It breathed farewells,
And whispered its final secret to me.

Leah Hill, a native of Illinois, is a writer living in northern Alabama. Studying family genealogy and walking in nature fuels much of her work. She is pursuing a graduate degree in Creative Writing and Literature through Harvard Extension School.

In Your Mother's Garden - Kate Maxwell

In your mother's garden, trees
-I can never remember their names -
stretch limbs above the old paling fence.

She has walked beneath pretty leaves
to point out flowering shrubs
perennials, rude weeds, but the names

fluttered away, escaping into pungent air.
Beyond the cracked slate pavers
of a well-pruned courtyard, busy with bees

that hover over lavender and rosemary
and worker ants on jittery march across
rough-edged stones, we stretch out

on soft grass. The big Elm shades us
this afternoon. I flick a lost and itchy ant
from my ankle and turn the page.

You lie, quietly snoring, like a well-fed dog
while your mother hangs out washing
peach sheets and pillow slips

still water-heavy in warm air. *Claret Ash.*
I remember now. A name to melt on
my tongue on this languid summer's day.

Kate Maxwell is yet another teacher with writing aspirations. She's been published and awarded in many Australian and International literary magazines. Kate's interests include film, wine, and sleeping. Her first poetry anthology is published with Interactive Publications, Brisbane.

The Rock, The Water - Matt Dennison

Walking wide-eyed, the child drops
to his knees, for the stream is all around
and flowing. He lifts the rock, the water
slurping its way beneath with thirsty relief,
washing cool the inhabitants who sigh
and tumble forth with amazing heads.
He catches some, damaging severely
with no cruelty, no knowing; he wants
them as they are to be wanted and no other.
He catches some more, now preciously aware,
glisteningly upheld. Satisfied, he stands.
Reaching the offered end of his journey
he marvels: I heard your call. I am here.
I will lift your rocks, pull back your bushes;
slide down your waterfalls, build me a dam.
I will return at night and stare into your eyes.
(Your warm spot is not yours; this I know.
You live by the fact of the sun; this I know.)
I will hear you move in the midnight water,
far from my touch — *O magic discovering*
of wondrous field, seemingly excellent,
perfect, and untouched! — I prefer my hand
in your side.

Matt Dennison is the author of Kind Surgery, from Urtica Press (Fr.) and Waiting for Better, from Main Street Rag Press. His work has appeared in Rattle, Bayou Magazine, Redivider, Natural Bridge, The Spoon River Poetry Review and Cider Press Review, among others.

Going Back - Matt Dennison

We placed the dead turtle
up high on the bank so we could find it again
with head and feet and snug tail gone
by way of the worm.

It happened quick, the disappearing inside.
But so much disappeared and so quickly
the shell simply fell in my hands
when next found.

So we scattered it,
some to the water, some to the mud —
most left in a pile of emptiness

next to something that was.

Matt Dennison is the author of Kind Surgery, from Urtica Press (Fr.) and Waiting for Better, from Main Street Rag Press. His work has appeared in Rattle, Bayou Magazine, Redivider, Natural Bridge, The Spoon River Poetry Review and Cider Press Review, among others.

Benediction - Carol Farnsworth

I take my coffee to the porch
to listen to the silence
between cricket chirps and bird song.
As a glow appears in the east, a solo bird call is heard,
followed by another and then a third.
The chorus swells.
My coffee cools as the rising sun warms my cheeks.
I smile at this morning benediction.

(Previously Published in The Weekly Avocet, Summer 2019)

Carol Farnsworth has been published in the Avocet, Magnets and Ladders, Plum Tree Tavern, Spirit Fire Review and Breath and Shadows. She has Published her first chap book, "Leaf Memories" about her experience with nature as a person with blindness. Born with glaucoma, Carol has experienced gradual vision loss all her life.

When The Sun Would Joyfully Rise
- Bobbi Sinha-Morey

A pure yellow goldfinch with
its tiny black markings flew away
from its perch on our neighbor's
fence before in its stillness I could
have savored its plump beauty,
wishing it would've stayed awhile
longer to alight on our water
fountain, wet its beak for a drink.
Now it's gone I could only imagine
other wildlife peering in our patio
garden so lovingly decorated by my
husband's hand, and nothing can
steal away my peace; my eyes falling
upon the agatized swirls of a rock
specimen he'd found, a mild wind
growing so silent I could hear
feathered kin overhead, and faraway
voices from other mobile homes across
the creek. It was just me, the sunlight
spilling through the glass roof above
me and for a minute I saw a feral
calico cat in all its colors, a rare sight
to see when everyone else had no pets
except for tiny dogs. I could sit here
all day with no one around to distract
me, glance at our verbena and primroses
that grew in pots, paving stones that
led halfway around and trellises for our
mums I loved to gaze upon from my
window when the sun would joyfully
rise, inviting me to come out again.

Bobbi Sinha-Morey's books are available at Amazon.com and her work has been nominated for The Best of the Net Anthology in 2015, 2018, 2020, and 2021. She's also been nominated for The Pushcart Prize in 2020.

Autumn Lamentations - Christina Laurie

The gangly spider
spreads her silk filaments
threading withered flowers
as autumn winds shake the blooms.
Feathery strands vibrate
as she lingers on the web
clinging to gossamer threads
that tremble as they
reflect silver moonlight.

How silent is the moonlight!
Grief has struck the heart
as it mourns among the roses
in the garden's back corner.
It dries up like petals
woven together with silken threads.

Weeping comes at night
tears flow alone
among silver-threaded blossoms.
Once holding life
bitter tears descend through autumn air
deserting a heart withered.
They sow grief into hardened earth.
\

Cape Cod resident Rev. Christina Laurie is the author of C is for Cape Cod *and* The Lobsters' Night Before Christmas, *two children's books. Her poetry collections include* Seasons Rising: A Collection of Haiku, Song of the Dancer, *and* Purr Poems: Kittens and Cats.

Piquant Whiffs - Sultana Raza

Fennel, black onions, or cumin seeds?
Lata was confused, about which to use
But as she inhaled their aroma deeply,
She was reminded of open fields
In the only village in Punjab she'd visited
As a precocious child, where they'd cooked out
Using real wood, a smoke-infused mélange of
Lentils, grain, cereals and spices.

As she took off the lids to smell all the spices
One by one, she felt less alone, as she thought
Of all the hard-working hands that had gone into harvesting,
Picking, cleaning, and packaging to get it to her.

Did the seeds remember the fresh air, the heat,
The scent of wet earth that had nurtured them
In their far-off infancy?

Her coriander and mint plants in their new plastic pots
Weren't so lucky after all.

But she made sure she hummed a soothing tune
While cooking near them. Did they nod in tune,
Stimulated by the steam,
Or was that just her wishful thinking
Bubbling up from nostalgia for no real reason at all?

Of Indian origin, Sultana Raza's poems, fiction, and non-fiction (100+ articles in English and French) have appeared in 100+ journals and anthologies, with an Honorable Mention in Glimmer Train Review. She's presented papers on Keats and Tolkien in international conferences, and has read her creative work in India, Europe and the USA.

Clam Digger - Timothy Dodd

She moves out onto the wet sand
when the horizon is between sun
and moon. Burrowers, she wants,
hiding from the coming tide, not
knowing of her hands, calloused,
knobby, for finding their fleeing.

They dig believing in wild universe,
carving out one's small patch, a want
to hold, to stay, like ours forever
in the shallows, mud, but a survival.

We reach in cold race for the catch,
in failure to look down at our own
grip, dawn, to the shore — our old
sustenance another's death. Gouging,
to grub, to scoop, to chase them
a burying, heading under, the grand
crashing in front of us, bearing down.

Timothy Dodd is from Mink Shoals, WV, and the author of Fissures, and Other Stories (Bottom Dog Press). His second collection of stories, Men in Midnight Bloom, is forthcoming (Cowboy Jamboree Press) as is a collection of poetry, Modern Ancient (High Window Press). Find a bit more writing on his 'Timothy Dodd, Writer' Facebook page.

Gardening is an Honor System - Deirdre Fagan

Broccoli goes with tomatoes,
tomatoes like onions,
strawberries remind me of you.

You on my hip, your tiny hand extended.

A few dollars placed in a jar.

May. You were barely two.
        You who had come into this world ginger-
        topped, screaming face crimson.

The fruit picked, then bitten, the cap handed back,
a small hand reaching – an exchange of red.
        Again. Again.

Strawberry all over your face and body,
        calyx discarded in a box at my feet
                your father then driving, grinning.

Your hips are now widening, your face pimpling.

First Father's ashes dangling from your neck.
Second Father kneeling beside you in the garden.

Adjusting the wild strawberries climbing unexpectedly,
        you dig barehanded in the dirt,
                and make room for new seedlings.

Deirdre Fagan is associate professor and coordinator of creative writing at Ferris State University. Fagan is the author of Find a Place for Me, (Pact Press, forthcoming, 2022), The Grief Eater, (Adelaide Books, 2020), and Have Love, (Finishing Line Press, 2019).

One Line a Day - Barbara Brooks

Words come like waves to the shore
but disappear as quickly as the ghost crab
scuttling to its hole. High tide's seaweed
hides the lines under the sargassum.
Common terns pluck metaphors
from the sea. Dropping the clamshells
on the road, the Laughing gull hopes for similes.
Wind blows the seafoam away along with this poem.

*Barbara Brooks, author of chapbooks, "The Catbird Sang", "A Shell to the Sea"
and Water Colors" has had poems accepted in "Tar River Poetry", "Peregrine",
"Silkworm".*

when all the weeds are gone - Angie Contini

I'll stop digging
I'll have time then
to search for something real
there are lovers
down here
buried alive
in the earth
there are wakes and vacancies and new world orders
the real soul of the world
lives beneath the ferns
in this feral, bacterial trove

Angie Contini is an experimental interdisciplinary artist and writer living in St Peters, with a PhD from the University of Sydney (2018). Specialising in the connection between art, nature and health, Angie works across a broad range of media, including photography, music, hand-cut collage, mixed media, theatre and poetry.

The Religion of Winter - Robert Rice

This morning as the world came into being
the frozen lake's surface had
nothing to say. This afternoon
it speaks with hollow, creaking sadness.
Roads are blocked.
Wind drags snow from the roof.
Among the branches, across a ghost sun,
nothing else moves.

My neighbor, wife gone from the virus,
carries his cambered shovel to the driveway,
breath leaving in white clouds,
and shifts the archived suffering
one shovelful at a time.
It gowns him in white, initiate newly born
to the religion of winter.
He nods. I turn away,
trudge through trackless afternoon.

Cold slurs toward evening.
Monotonic light, empty as a ring,
absorbs the discriminated world
and darkness, finally,
opens into silence so complete
love, itself, must call from it.
Pierced by an owl's talons, a rabbit,
in agony and muted rapture,
feels it, too. Amen.

Robert Rice's stories and poems have appeared or are forthcoming in various literary magazines, including Hayden's Ferry, New Letters, The North American Review, The Saint Ann's Review, and West Wind Review. He has also published three novels, including The Last Pendragon and The Nature of Midnight. He lives in Montana.

The Minutiae of Nature - Gregory Tullock

The minutiae of nature
Capture my eye
And captivate my heart

The tiny things of the world
Contain such beauty and wonder
Such intricacy and richness of detail

Moth antennae
As thin as baby eyelashes
Fine gossamer webs
On the grass
The delicate spores
Tucked on the underside of a fern

The smaller the insect, the fungus, the flower
The greater the concentration of the divine

Gregory Tullock resides in Asheville, North Carolina. He is a father, mailman, beekeeper, hiker, and poet. His writing is inspired by time spent in nature, a rich dream life, and an appreciation for Taoist philosophy.

Open Window - Josie Rozell

Clasping my hands behind my back,
I survey the sights from the kitchen window
and breathe deeply the wind that docks
from the mountain tops tucked in clouds.
All is fair, if one counts birds and lemon trees
against the straying plastic trash kicked up
by flattened car tires and pulsing hydrants.
The neighbour boys clatter skateboards
against the stretched asphalt, heat dust
wavering between ground and sky.
Crisped linen shirts wiggle freely
on laundry lines, and I count that as good, too.

The bread cools next to me on the countertop
and quietly, I close the window.

Josie Rozell is a Hawai'i-based indie poet and essayist. She is the author of Articulated Soul, a collection of poems and collage from five areas of the world, and is at work on her second book of poetry, Deep Breath, featuring sonnets and surrealist collage.

The Zen of Looking Up - Ellen Lager

Overhead, the cottonwood
surrenders its seed
to rivers of air.
Hollow-boned orioles
and goldfinches, maple samaras
attired in wings,
sail into a musical flight show
of an uncharted destination.
Gulls float the shoreline,
unburden wailing calls
into a vortex of clouds
where the great blue heron
trysts with the infinite
between apricot horizons
and Arcturus, the first star.

Ellen Lager's poems have been published in The MacGuffin, Neologism, Sheila-Na-Gig, Encore, Litbreak, and Sanskrit, as well as various anthologies. Her favorite place to write is at a lake cabin in northern MN with her husband, two dogs and two cats.

Luna - Carol Grametbauer

Climbing to the top of the ridge
on a July morning, we find
on the street the scattered wings
of a luna moth, pastel green
against the dark asphalt –
a discovery we've made
a half-dozen times before,
spring to mid-summer, always
in the same location. Rather
than let them be ruined by tires

I gather all four, a burden so light
I can barely feel it; study
the delicate twist of the tails,
the sepia-bordered eyespots,
as flawless as if stenciled
by some incorporeal artist.
They leave on my fingers a gloss
of powder, like fairy dust,
the color of moonlight,
testimony that a singular magic

still exists in this struggling world,
waits at the top of the hill
to be found again and again.

Carol Grametbauer is the author of two chapbooks: *Homeplace* (Main Street Rag, 2018), and *Now & Then* (Finishing Line Press, 2014). Her poems have appeared in numerous journals including *Appalachian Heritage, Connecticut River Review, Pine Mountain Sand & Gravel,* and *The Sow's Ear Poetry Review,* and in several anthologies.

Spiderscape - Jack Granath

What creature
makes cobwebs
like these
on cedar chips
and leaves
them to shimmer
in the light
morning wind?
They look like
distant lakes,
but ghost ones
superimposed
on the fragrant

chaos of this

pregnable ground

Jack Granath is a librarian in Kansas.

Antares - Anne Pinkerton

You're on the lookout for stars,
and only one shows itself
when the day darkens,
but it is so bright,
it demands to be witnessed, it burns hot
through deep charcoal smudges of clouds
and a backdrop of deepening indigo
muting every minute.

The trees bleed into ink drawings,
and this one light in the sky is
as red and distinct as the planet
it is not.

You open your star app
and aim it at the horizon,
find the bright spot's name,
research its data:
Fifteenth brightest —
a supergiant, yes, but also
actually double stars, merged,
or what their convergence appears as,
together, binary.

To be so vibrant —
twelve times brighter than
the sun, with a heat you can nearly feel
here on earth, it's really no surprise
it takes two.

Anne Pinkerton studied poetry at Hampshire College and received an MFA in creative nonfiction from Bay Path University. Her writing has been published in Sunlight Press, Hippocampus Magazine, River Teeth's 'Beautiful Things,' Entropy Magazine, Modern Loss, and Ars Medica, among others. Her memoir will be published by Vine Leaves Press in 2023.

Through the Night - Christopher Woods

by dusk is was done,
the cow gave birth
in the low pasture
away from the winter wind.
this is when the vultures
descended, black feathery angels
intent on the feast of afterbirth.

but as the sky darkened
the angels wanted more
and began to swoop low
pace greedily about the ground
near the still wet calf
in a smaller and smaller circle.

darkness enclosing them all,
the other cows came close
and formed a ring
around the new calf,
keeping the buzzards at bay.
they stood that way for hours,
hulking silhouettes in the night,
dumb, unthinking beasts
we hold dominion over.

Christopher Woods is a writer and photographer who lives in Chappell Hill, Texas. His poetry chapbook, What Comes, What Goes, *was published by Kelsay Books.*

Point of Ambiguity - Laurie Rosen

On Vermont trails:
two blue blazes, one
above the other,
on tree trunks and boulders,
alert hikers to pay attention,
keep on the sharply

curving path.
Yet, more often than not
the double lines don't puncture
the poems or predicaments
crowding my head
and I overlook

the turn.
For a time, bushwhacking
thickening brush, every step
increasingly difficult,
I wander the wrong way.

Still, I might encounter
a patch of white birch —
yellow leaves shimmering
in early autumn sunlight,
bunches of chicken-of-the-woods,
a thicket of wild blueberries —
for my picking alone.

Then this: clarity, a pivot
and I retrace my steps,
heading in the direction
I mean to go--guided

by blue blazes from those
who came before.

Laurie Rosen is a lifelong New Englander. Her poems have appeared in The London Reader; The Muddy River Poetry Review; Oddball Magazine; Soul-Lit; The New Verse News; Zig Zag Magazine and elsewhere.

Grandfather Tree – Don Magin

Stronger than it was
weaker than it will be.
More gnarled than it used to be
less knotted than it will become.

It is as old as I.

Rooted.
Grounded to provide a stable base
from which to reach to the stars.

I wonder

does it wonder,
what will become of
the seeds of its seeds?

Don Magin retired from careers as research chemist and science/math teacher. He and Margaret, his wife of 53 years, live in Bon Air, Virginia. He has had stories and poems published in Grand Magazine, Guide Magazine, Central Virginia Poetry Bard Magazine, Sylvia, and other online and print publications.

Fog Grove - Diane Webster

Fog transforms aspen grove
into ocean of seaweed.
Imagine trees swaying
on cloudy waves undulating
back and forth –
rhythmic vertigo.

Like National Geographic
cameras impersonating
eyes at the scene
so a hand reaches
for steering wheel,
solid in its gravity power
as headlights view fog
lift into canopy of trees.

Diane Webster's goal is to remain open to poetry ideas in everyday life, nature or an overheard phrase and to write. Diane enjoys the challenge of transforming images into words to fit her poems. Her work has appeared in "Home Planet News Online," "North Dakota Quarterly," "Talking River Review" and other literary magazines.

Winter - Zara Raab

The river's running freer now
though birch have laid their shadow-slats
aslant the snow, their branches making
patterned shapes against the sky.
A stiffened snow collars the banks,
while new lays windward stripes on trees,
sweet birch and lighter paper birch,
and fills the elbow-crooks of limbs.

Overhead the predators
of grey-tailed voles now wheel and turn;
linen beds the cobble, smooth
and white; I crunch along a path,
pine-dark, then come once more at last
to sky turned purple-blue, and field,
whose cobbled earth in rows rest under snow.
The hawks have flown and cold is wedged
in all the crevices of rock.

*Zara Raab will release two of her books, Swimming the Eel and Fracas &
Asylum, in a combined New Edition later this year. Her work, including book
reviews, as well as poems, has appeared in The Hudson Review, Verse Daily,
River Styx, West Branch, Arts & Letters, Critical Flame, Prime Number, Raven
Chronicles, and The Dark Horse. She recently joined the Powow River Poets
north of Boston.*

Forgetting to Close the Gate
- Rachel Elion Baird

When the clouds grew heavy
I gathered with the others, to watch
in silence,
those ponies and white goats
that go unclaimed on this island –
they are the wild things
that touch the mountain
without effort or knowledge of what they hold.
I can hear them running in the night
when my eyes are closed in sleep:
the herd grazing by the gate
just outside the flower garden,
the ponies running past
close enough to touch,
you and I laughing a little too loud,
following the small brown sheep,
finding their fleece in clumps on the path,
stopping just short of the square house.
In the storm I dream of trees falling backwards
against the old stone wall,
laid down to make a bed for all our moving shadows,
freighted hooves sounding in the dark,
like the prayers that cross my lips,
go unheard into that black rain path,
those clouds.

Rachel Elion Baird's poems are visual confessionals, unfolding stories through descriptive imagery. Her work appears in numerous publications including New Millennium Writings, SouthLight, and Into the Void. A member of the Edinburgh School of Poets, Baird is the author of published poetry collections: Uplands, and Valentines and other Tragedies.

A Healing at Walden Pond - Douglas J. Lanzo

I still recall the first time
I beheld Walden Pond.
It was a brisk September morning, many years ago,
the first year of college cross-country season,
when our team bus came to a stop
in an autumnal forest in Concord,
parking within eyesight of the replica
of Henry David Thoreau's tiny chimneyed home,
overlooking the shores of a vast lake.

Gazing upon soft clouds,
my eyes tranquilly sailed with them
across its surface, smooth as fresh-blown glass.
It gazed back at me
with smiling radiance,
welling up from pure blue depths
of ancient wisdom,
a kettle lake,
settled by the weight of a glacier
pondering its beauty,
entire trees, robed in mapled red,
reflecting from its placid waters.

Suddenly aware of each breath,
I felt my lungs fill with forest air,
tinged by the scent of evergreens.
Something indescribable within me
became lighter, lifting with my chest,
awakening a longing for
something more simple and good.

When my coach bid those
suffering from ailments to
wade into the cool waters of
Walden Pond, I followed,
beckoned by the healing
I felt inside.

An award-winning and featured American poet published in Vita Brevis Press'
bestselling 2021 Poetry Anthology, Brought to Sight & Swept Away, whose
first novel, The Year of the Bear, is forthcoming, 178 of Doug's poems have been
published in 43 literary publications since 2020 across 10 countries and 5
continents. To read more poems authored by Doug or his twin sons or to pre-
order his novel, please kindly visit his website at douglaslanzo.com.

Plume - Aleda Estlin

Setting sun, across me, silent, sketching a loss.
Its reds melt behind my back into the noise of the high grass.

I look elsewhere.
The wind gilds the air in dusk
and it billows through me,
gaining ground over the landscape
beyond the water.

I stand facing the white hotel.
Wind moves like a danseuse,
its hips synchronised with nightfall,
left to right,
right to left,
faint light glides in waves,
gradient, invoking my own twilight.

Slyly, it makes the picture vibrant;
the short fences,
the hydrangeas,
the windy porches drenched with
the green abysmal stench of seawater
seize the stage, sweeping my sight.
They don their dress &
braid with night - a lush
theatre of diminishment.

And just before collapsing into slumber,
the zealous lines & curbs & depths of everything
shine in the dusk like glass eyes on doll faces with loose lids;
throb as they flap in dashes, up and down,
looking at the world dipping in sleep.

The day falls flat among the rocks of night.
The bulrush shushes; dull echo.

I watch the shadow play, up, at the entrance.
The drowsy clan of sand concludes, aghast, its rant.
Blunt yellows turn the shore to dross and go nocturnal.

The people seem erratic in the coastal draft.
Their splendid mimic draws the drape of shade.
And shaded they adorn the night, blind bustle.

Their echoes twin the passing on of life,
the setting sun consuming on the shore,
the birth of moon, me, waiting
in the breath of night,
wide-eyed cocoon,
so silent.

I hear the whoosh of lips
lulling the world to sleep.
I gaze far out into the gleam of night
to watch stars puff. I see them spread
over the face of God, bright freckles.
With curls and hoops,
She reins the sky above;
She casts no shadows.

Aleda Estlin writes poetry and creative non-fiction. She holds a BA in Comparative Literature and an MA in Cultural Studies. Her interests tap into the fields of literature, visual culture, fashion, psychology, and spirituality. She's often inspired by birds, water, and secluded places. Currently, she's experimenting with photopoems.

By the Cape Cod Sea - Pamela Ahlen

Here at the far end
the sea-salt smell, the scallop shells,
one gull in squalling interjection,
reprising all the silky, coarse
and rocky sands that edged blustery,
even peaceable seas —
how lost we found ourselves to be.
Here by the Cape Cod sea the tide ebbs benign,
two old sharks in bloodless capitulation,
or maybe harbor seals in quiet appreciation.

Pamela Ahlen is the author of the chapbook Gather Every Little Thing (Finishing Line Press) and a collaborative chapbook with poet Anne Bower Getting it Down on Paper, Shaping a Friendship (Orchard Street Press). She lives in rural Vermont where she shares her dirt road with the occasional bear.

A sportsman - DS Maolalai

he'd lost a good hook
in a small rainbow
trout. and he was 16
and was only
a sportsman, and that
only barely - no killer
of things. he didn't
like gutting or that
so much either.
and he took the fish
home and then threw it
away, in the grass
by the hedge and some
ivy. the dog found it
later and swallowed it -
started acting odd quickly.
was sick for a couple of days.

DS Maolalai has been nominated nine times for Best of the Net and seven times for the Pushcart Prize. His poetry has been released in two collections, "Love is Breaking Plates in the Garden" (Encircle Press, 2016) and "Sad Havoc Among the Birds" (Turas Press, 2019)

Cyclical - Pamela Ahlen

All the leaves left the trees,
the coreopsis and hydrangea went to bed.

I mourn the worn-out things —
the last rutabaga, the scarecrow,

the close-mouthed brook,
everything said that needed to be said,

our words
stored like old rakes and hoes in the garden shed.

Autumn pulled down its shade,
done-in sun squeezing out anemic rays.

You say it won't last this way forever.
After all,

earth's giving us another run-around. And
the sun simply turned its face away — pretending.

Pamela Ahlen is the author of the chapbook Gather Every Little Thing (Finishing Line Press) and a collaborative chapbook with poet Anne Bower Getting it Down on Paper, Shaping a Friendship (Orchard Street Press). She lives in rural Vermont where she shares her dirt road with the occasional bear.

Surrender - Lisa Romano Licht

Helplessly they drift
to grassy earth,
already scattered
with casualties--
bright yellow, scarred
black and brown

Some lie twitching
sun lighting their veins
delicate as a child's;
others surrender skyward
flat and lifeless

A deliberate wind triggers
more tumbled gold
past crowded limbs:
rustling, sighing in the fall
before the landing, soundless

The rest hang panicked
in the trees, urgent
whispering passed between
unready for self-sacrifice

Lisa Romano Licht's work has appeared in The Westchester Review, Ovunque Siamo, Mom Egg Review, Capsule Stories and other journals, and was selected for The Year's Best Dog Stories 2021 and the Train River COVID-19 Anthology. She holds an MA in Writing from Manhattanville College. Find her on Twitter: @LRLwrites

Lantern in the Woods - *Cynthia d'Este*

This morning
beyond the windowpane
a raft of box elder trees
has yellowed overnight,
set a lantern in the woods.

Now, in afternoon, a mist
up from the still-summering gulf
bathes the gilded branches
with autumnal sheen.

Antiqued sails of milkweed
ride tall-rigged through the wild fields
on bowed and sinuous waves.
All is still, after the quiet
exhalation of the pines.

Does age come suddenly
or in the guise of seasons –
a safe, slow savagery that hides
in the belly all along

close to the breath
but hungry in its hollow,
out now stealing light
for the era of no return.

Cynthia d'Este's poetry has appeared in magazines, newspapers, regional anthologies and small press editions across the U.S. Her lyric works have been composed and performed on stage by the Milwaukee Chamber Orchestra and Present Music, Milwaukee's internationally acclaimed new music ensemble.

Among the Shasta Daisies - J.R. Solonche

Among the Shasta daisies,
in the middle of them,
a center of black-eyed susans,
surrounded by the white
of the daises, their yellow-gold
circle is an eye.
                    I tell you,
as I get nearer and nearer to
the way things are, more and more
am I convinced that the earth
knows more than it will ever say.

*Nominated for the National Book Award and twice-nominated for the Pulitzer
Prize, J.R. Solonche is the author of 26 books of poetry and coauthor of another.
He lives in the Hudson Valley.*

Inside Out - Diane Webster

Black tree branches stretch
across the sky view
in solder separation
on a stained-glass window
vivid with sunshine
viewed from the inside out.

Sparrows sing
from tree limb pews
in hallelujah chorus
shaking leaves in upraised praise
while bumblebees buzz amen
climbing inside out
snapdragon blossoms.

Diane Webster's goal is to remain open to poetry ideas in everyday life, nature or an overheard phrase and to write. Diane enjoys the challenge of transforming images into words to fit her poems. Her work has appeared in "Home Planet News Online," "North Dakota Quarterly," "Talking River Review" and other literary magazines.

Benediction for a Fallen Pine - Ellen Lager

Down the shore, a white pine toppled into water
in a thunderstorm overnight.

Over the years, it became our focal point, a balance beam
where kids frolicked and fell, dived from its sturdy trunk,

cast lines and drifted near in kayaks.
Sunfish and perch carved the water in its shadow.

Safe haven for mallards and loons in summer,
bench respite for snowshoe hikers in winter,

the algae bloomed ochre and orange, warmed the gray
of sunless days. We captured it in the lapse of seasons

with a photographer's eye, its bark chipped and thinned in waves,
its needles dissolved, steadfast limbs declined.

Small-mouth bass still shelter there.

Ellen Lager's poems have been published in The MacGuffin, Neologism, Sheila-Na-Gig, Encore, Litbreak, and Sanskrit, as well as various anthologies. Her favorite place to write is at a lake cabin in northern MN with her husband, two dogs and two cats.

Wonderment of Zion - Suzanne Cottrell

Gazed up at sheer Navajo sandstone,
translucent quartz granules
glistened in Utah sunlight.
Sparkling stones created
treasured memories.

Lofty cliffs of cream, ochre, rose, cocoa
formed staircase across the horizon of
Zion National Park.
Rocks wept as water seeped
through porous layers.

Virgin River gouged sedimentary rock,
carved gorges, grottoes, arches.
Competing fault lines produced escarpments,
wonderment of geological
layers, markers of time.

Canyon views captivated,
Checkerboard Mesa mystified
with its cross-hatching cracks.
Surly shadows danced on rock faces,

We sought refuge at desert camp site.
Sparce hackberry, ash, cotton
woods provided shade.
Towering sentinels, Watchman's Rock,

Three Patriarchs guarded our solitude,
graced by Peregrine falcons, bald eagles.
Our spirits soared freely,
intrigued by the unusual
landscape of Colorado Plateau.

Suzanne Cottrell, an outdoor enthusiast and retired teacher, lives with her husband in rural Piedmont North Carolina. She is the author of three poetry chapbooks: Gifts of the Seasons, Autumn and Winter; Gifts of the Seasons, Spring and Summer; and Scarred Resilience.

Dinner and Conversation with a Jack Rabbit
- Rose Menyon Heflin

Amid the towering rock formations
and formidable, punishing boulders
surrounding my campsite
in Joshua Tree National Park,
a jack rabbit stares back at me
in careful observation,
its brown eyes watchful
in silent conversation,
its cleverly camouflaged fur
a lustrous tawny color.
Deeming me and my camera not a threat,
it resumes munching
on a desperately thirsty desert plant,
its long ears erect,
stretched as far as they
seem to be able to go,
alert for any other potential dangers.

Of course, it would finish its dinner.
It was I who had invaded its home,
setting up a large and imposing
temporary one of my own ,
chatting loudly,
stirring up dust
as I trekked large footprints
through the loose desert soil,
disturbing,
disturbing,
disturbing,
unapologetically in awe.

But what can I do,
except join the rabbit at dinner,
muttering to him quietly
and receiving pointed looks in return,
store my trash
in the vehicle to minimize
my horrid disturbance,
pick up my camera,
and resume my
mostly non-verbal conversation
with the jack rabbit?

Rose Menyon Heflin is an award-winning poet from Madison, WI. Her work has appeared in numerous journals spanning four continents. One of her poems was performed by a local dance troupe. Recent and forthcoming publications include DREICH, Fauxmoir, Feral, MacQueen's Quinterly, sPARKLE & bLINK, and Tangled Locks Journal's MoonBites.

Ducks - Jack Granath

Two ducks huddle on a log,
as if afraid to get
their bright, webbed feet wet,
and I cruise by, unlike them
today, stomping through the woods,
but the sunset will wipe us out,
and tomorrow I may be them,
feet up off the floor in my office,
each knock at the door a splash of cold water,
and they could be me,
ducks in the woods on a good day
or a little part of one.

Jack Granath is a librarian in Kansas.

Salt Lick in Moonlight - Joel Savishinsky

The faint chorus of stars,
singing not to us but to
one another. The ratio of
their orbits long a subject
of magic and math,
their harmonies still lost
in the slow light of dusk.

Above the eastern horizon
of the Adirondacks, a density
of them wells up, a salt lick
in moonlight, patient for creatures
that hide in constellations before
making their hunger known.

How will we ever know
the seasons of our lives
if we do not open
our mouths to the heavens,
or question why it is easier
to write a poem about love than
pen the lines of a love poem.

Joel Savishinsky is an anthropologist and gerontologist, whose book, Breaking the Watch: The Meanings of Retirement in America, won the Gerontology Society's book-of-the-year prize. His poetry, fiction and essays have appeared in The Avocet, Beyond Words, Cirque, Metafore, Poetry Quarterly, SLANT, Toho Journal, and Windfall. He lives in Seattle.

Balm - Sherry Poff

In the waning light of a winter sky
bright-rimmed clouds suspend
between blue and branches.
And I remember my mother--
all my child's heart knew
of tenderness
until this day when light drips
as honey from the clouds,
pools on the horizon like a promise.

Sherry Poff writes in and around Ooltewah, Tennessee. She holds an M.A. in writing from The University of Tennessee at Chattanooga and is a member of the Chattanooga Writers' Guild. Her work has appeared recently in Raconteur Review, Heart of Flesh, *and* The Chattanooga Pulse.

Mid October - Connie Jordan Green

Listen to rain rattling yellow poplar leaves,
its patter on porch roof, a song sung to departing
birds, goodbye, goodbye whispered to corn stalks

where only a few weeks ago summer tassels frenzied
the bees. Across the valley mountains shoulder into fog,
hold their summits up for whatever sun may shine

before day's end. Earth drinks in this rare soaking,
asters and crown beard bowing their autumn hues
to the gray of this day. We pull out the soup pot, slice

carrots, potatoes, onions — those denizens of the dark
regions of the garden — sear them to tenderness or
translucence, flavors bubbling through tomatoes we add,

then a sprinkling of salt, fistful of basil, thyme, magic
of oregano — this mid-October day with her comforts
seducing us before the dark that waits ahead.

Connie Jordan Green lives on a farm in East Tennessee where she writes and gardens. She is the author of award-winning novels for young people, poetry chapbooks, and two poetry collections. Her poetry has been nominated for Pushcart Prizes. She frequently leads writing workshops.

The Spirit of the Earth - Walt Page

When I walk through the woods
I can feel the spirit of the earth
I feel close to Heaven
as gentle breezes caress me

I love to feel a gentle rain
as it washes away my pain
I dream about the sea
as I wait to be set free

I love to feel the sunshine's
warm light healing me
and when I look up at the sky
I want to spread my wings and fly

I hear the singing of the birds
and try to put it all in words
the spirit of the earth
helps to ease my pain

Walt is just a romantic old rock and roll drummer, US Air Force veteran and open-heart surgery survivor, living the country life in Tennessee and writing his poetry on love, life, music and whatever comes to mind. He's published in Visual Verse, Vita Brevis and Slasher Magazine. His work also appears in two Poetry Anthologies from Vita Brevis Press.

Wave Analysis - John C. Mannone

There's always something we can take away
when we stop to study nature, even the dead
things like river water, the way it bends, yields
to the breeze—a patchwork of quilted waves
holding secrets of their motion, the glitters
of sun glued to dark green slopes betraying
the tug of moon, whispers of wind. Slapping
water, a boat rounds the corner, and it's gone
except for its wake. I awaken to the splash
of light and dark, and wonder about the shades
of meaning between us. It all depends on our
perception of the depth of these troubled waters
and where the shoals are, where we can stand
and not drown.

John C. Mannone has poems in Windhover, North Dakota Quarterly, Poetry South, and others. He was awarded a Jean Ritchie Fellowship (2017) in Appalachian literature and served at the celebrity judge for the National Federation of State Poetry Societies (2018). He's the poetry editor for Abyss & Apex. A retired physics professor, John lives in Knoxville, Tennessee.

Sunrise - John C. Mannone

The geodesic dome triangles the dusk,
storm windows still glassing the dark
landscape. Soon, colors will shine through
—hues of Georgia red clay, Macon.

Windows pummeled, scratched from sand
churning in dust devil's dance last night
(and for a long time before that), let the hazy
sun splinter through the crazing.

I miss the Rayleigh-scattered skies,
water vapor bouncing all the blue away
to leave the flaming reds and golds
of sunrise, but here, so far from home

despite the faithful beauty of the blaze
of blue sunrises—because of ubiquitous
rusty sand absorbing all the red—I ache
for you on these cold & lonely mornings
on Mars.

John C. Mannone has poems in Windhover, North Dakota Quarterly, Poetry South, and others. He was awarded a Jean Ritchie Fellowship (2017) in Appalachian literature and served at the celebrity judge for the National Federation of State Poetry Societies (2018). He's the poetry editor for Abyss & Apex. A retired physics professor, John lives in Knoxville, Tennessee.

The Egg - Jacqueline Garlitos

Under the maple, the ground
tinged with ice, an egg
so pale — as if the color
had winged skyward.
A slight smear
of green afterbirth
all that remained
of its mother. Now it lay
alone. I took it home, held it
to the light looking for the bird
within. Only shadow
peered back. I packed it
in rabbits' feet and stole
my father's desk lamp.
The gooseneck bent over
the egg, like a mother, like
a god, as if life could walk
down the rungs of light. Each day
I peered at the shadow
inside, until one day I knew it
for what it was. And like its mother,
like its god, I hung my head
and wept.

Last year, during the pandemic, Jacqueline Garlitos and her husband moved from New Jersey to Idaho in order to have more time to write. She received her MFA in 2004. After graduating, she became a finalist/semifinalist for several national awards.

A Suite for Spring - Stephen Ruffus

With the light coming earlier now
Every morning I am in perfect step
With my own shadow
Where new possibilities await me.

*

We met in the spring. The coming season
Will be shaded with conversations recalling
Gentle walks engraved in memory
When our skin was as brown as the earth.

*

Our mothers are aged in the extreme.
We are out of step and slipping out
Of time. The notes on the kitchen table
Are the daily reminders.

*

It snowed yesterday presenting us with
Another path to follow. The bright sun
Against the whiteness may have blinded us
Yet awakened us too from our slumber.

for Kathy

Stephen Ruffus's work has appeared or is forthcoming in the Valparaiso Poetry Review, the American Journal of Poetry, Eunoia Review, Red Eft Review, The Stray Branch, Hotel Amerika, Vita Brevis, and The Shore. He has studied poetry at Colorado State University, the University of California at Irvine, and the University of Utah. He is from New York City and resides in Salt Lake City.

The Smallest Birds - Tricia Gates Brown

Awe as I watch the smallest birds:
lesser goldfinches, firm as fists,
Anna's hummingbirds, the field

sparrows, crushing my throat
like grief. Heads tilt: "How
interesting *this*, how interesting *that*";

legs twitch like boys on a playground.
Last week I found a sparrow near
dead, half breathing, eyes open

and terror-stricken. I wanted to save him,
extend one finger of comfort. His pebble
eyes folded in a cradle

of new grass.
Sadness catches me.
I do not want to die.

Tricia Gates Brown's poems have appeared in various publications including Portland Review, Mason Street Literary Magazine, GEEZ Magaine, and Vita Brevis. Living on a farm in Yamhill, Oregon, she writes and edits, and dotes on a four-legged menagerie. She is author of the debut novel Wren (Frederick Press 2021).

In the Valley of Light - Ivor Steven

The cold winds of change
Blow down from the mountain range
Gathering up lost souls estranged

Rescuing them from the forest of shadows
And release them into the sunny valleys of tomorrow

Where there is light, there is colour
Where there is colour, there is energy
Where there is energy, there is life

Ivor was formerly an Industrial Chemist, then a Plumber, and has been writing for 20 years. He is a member of Geelong Writer Inc (Australia), a team member with the on-line blog-site 'Go Dog Go Café (America), and is a writer for the 'Coffee House Writers Magazine (America).

Lay of the Land - Eamon O'Caoineachan

O Leyland — Leyland cypress trees, lay across
our road, lay across our land, so we can keep
our family home, so we can always keep
our ancient and ancestral meadowland.
Last night, a wild Atlantic storm blew over

five Leyland cypress trees that now lie across
our road, lie across our land, uprooted,
they lay on the straight road — wooden kerbstone cross.
My father, mother, sister, brother, and I,
we are the fallen trees that laid, lay, and lie

but it's not meant to be, only meant to cry
for a stolen home, for a stolen land.
Art was long in the long wood and life there
was short, but that is the lay of the land,
when you lose your home, when you lose your land

a family can forgive, but can never
forget, or understand — so steal our home, steal our land,
but as long as just one Leyland cypress stands
through every storm evergreen trees withstand —
we will always lay there — we will always stand.

Eamon O'Caoineachan is a poet, originally from Co. Donegal, Ireland, but living in Houston, Texas. His work is published in The Ekphrastic Review, Vita Brevis Press, East-West Literary Forum, Lothlorien Poetry Journal, Prometheus Dreaming, Madness Muse Press, and the University of St. Thomas's literary magazines, Thoroughfare and Laurels. He is the recipient of The Robert Lee Frost-Vince D'Amico Poetry Award and the Rev. Edward A. Lee Endowed Scholarship in English at the University of St. Thomas, Houston. He has his MLA in English Literature and is his first poetry collection, Dolphin Ghosts, was published in Spring 2021.

Pondering the women who, given no choice, mourned leisure - Tricia Gates Brown

Noticing the dogs make a blanket of sun,
I move out under the bee tree, hear them
barely for the sound of lawn mower, bird
song, creek song, jitter of bamboo chime.

But the bees sidle close, outline the page
where I write, asking, what is there to say
but the blue of forget-me-nots, a bow
on the horizon, tip-toeing on this April

day? Moondust euphorbia, raspberry peony,
hands to the Lord, erysimum navel orange,
stretching side-long to the violet of hyacinth?
Even the aspenwood risks its leafing. Let

the wind kiss you, the bee-monk says, let it
always take longer, this kissing. Dog slinks past,
its fur a warm invitation, and I,
stubborn as a beam, finally give in.

Is it not better to lie in a blanket of sun?

Tricia Gates Brown's poems have appeared in various publications including Portland Review, Mason Street Literary Magazine, GEEZ Magaine, and Vita Brevis. Living on a farm in Yamhill, Oregon, she writes and edits, and dotes on a four-legged menagerie. She is author of the debut novel Wren (Frederick Press 2021).

A Kind of Church - Chris Wood

Moonlight shivers,
layers the darkness
in gray and silver.

My thoughts scatter
into the wood
spiraling upward.

Breezes brushing my skin,
I close my eyes, lift my face
toward the sky,

confide my troubles
to heaven, stars winking
in understanding.

Leaves chanting against the blackness,
endless whispers
soothing a mind full of worry.

Chris Wood resides in Tennessee with her husband and several fur babies. Her work has appeared in several journals and publications, including Poetry Quarterly, Haiku Journal, American Diversity Report, *and* Quill and Parchment.

Autumn Blaze - Sterling Warner

Under frost covered leaves
veins arc like petrified rainbows
spreading midrib stalks
disappearing into a semblance
of nine serrated lobes, tinged
with icy cane sugar granules
preserve broad maple mittens

smashed into mother earth like flowers
pressed between pages of a Russian novel.

Inanimate mementos forsake
acrylic cellular blankets & cuddle
amid stiff cellulose fibers laced
with talcum power. Comfortable.
Secure. Almond-like odors mix scents
of sour vanilla & baby's breath
after breastfeeding — woody camphor

emerging as footsteps crunch foliage
& slip on slimy yellow gastropod trails.

Author, poet, educator, Sterling Warner's works have appeared in literary magazines, journal and anthologies such Ekphrastic Review, Vita Brevis Anthology I & II, and Fib. His six poetry books include Without Wheels, ShadowCat, Edges, Rags & Feathers, Serpent's Tooth, and Flytraps plus Masques: Flash Fiction & Short Stories.

Controlled Burn - James P. Daigler

Smoke signal rising, ash
Black against the winter sky.
Over treetops, over housetops
Epicenter: Park.
Well, there you go, last
Vestige of great prairie
Wilderness, encircled,
Suffocated by urban sprawl.
It's for your health, they say.
A cure for the disease we caused.
Typical.
Are you erased or reborn in the flames?
Phoenix or forgotten?
In spring, you might flourish,
Reclaim a sliver of what was stolen.
More likely, you'll be dirt, wasted
Space, waiting for some false Eden
To take your place.

James P. Daigler is an emerging writer of short fiction, essays, and poetry. Communication, storytelling, and humanity's impact on the world are common themes in his work. When not writing, James is an English teacher in Madison, WI, working to inspire the next generation of readers and writers.

Water Lilies - Ken Gierke

I move beside the shore,
water creased by the bow before me,
caressed by the paddle beside me.
Startled, a heron takes flight
from a fallen tree at water's edge,
its wings a faint whisper in the silence.
Paddle still, I drift past a willow
into a floating carpet of green.
Pink and white lilies nod as they part.
I pause in the stillness,
Monet's vision spread before me.
At peace, amid peace.

Ken Gierke writes poetry primarily in free verse and haiku. He has been published at Vita Brevis, The Ekphrastic Review, Silver Birch Press, Amethyst Review, and Eunoia Review. His poetry is included in two anthologies from Vita Brevis Press, Pain & Renewal and Brought to Sight and Swept Away, as well as in easing the edges: a collection of everyday miracles, an anthology edited by D Ellis Phelps. His work can be found at his blog: rivrvlogr.wordpress.com.□

The Raker's Progress - Joel Savishinsky

The last leaves on the maple
have seen the future and are
determined it won't happen
to them: the gray faces of
this already dis-spirited century,
our own meager hopes,
the ever-ready compromises
with integrity. They have
witnessed my grandchildren
playing among the dead,
kicking up bones into dusty
clouds. The leaves' translucent
fingers dangle from limbs,
signaling to let the wintry
world have its way. We will
wait, they sign, and watch until
spring forces us out by its touch
on our stubborn stems. This is
still our tree, our tree of life,
a silent citadel that can guard
frail soldiers and doomed relics
left behind by fortune, covering
the retreat of sisters and brothers
who've sought refuge in the slow,
subtle warmth of earth's decay.

Joel Savishinsky is an anthropologist and gerontologist, whose book, Breaking the Watch: The Meanings of Retirement in America, won the Gerontology Society's book-of-the-year prize. His poetry, fiction and essays have appeared in The Avocet, Beyond Words, Cirque, Metafore, Poetry Quarterly, SLANT, Toho Journal, and Windfall. He lives in Seattle.

Downstream - Ken Gierke

Paddle slices the surface,
kayak glides, my wake
the only waves visible.

Cardinal calls. Turtles bask
in morning sun. Eagle lands
in towering sycamore.

Heron recedes downstream,
it's wings stately
in their slow steady beat.

Rising. Falling.
Subject to season.
Wings and water, as one.

Always, it flows,
meandering, as life will do.
River holds all, and more.

Ken Gierke writes poetry primarily in free verse and haiku. He has been published at Vita Brevis, The Ekphrastic Review, Silver Birch Press, Amethyst Review, and Eunoia Review. His poetry is included in two anthologies from Vita Brevis Press, Pain & Renewal and Brought to Sight and Swept Away, as well as in easing the edges: a collection of everyday miracles, an anthology edited by D Ellis Phelps. His work can be found at his blog: rivrvlogr.wordpress.com.□

To the Spider Mites Infesting My Bonsai
- James P. Daigler

I forgive
You and your destructive habits,
The webs and specks you stash
On the bottom of my leaves
Won't wash away. Are those
Your eggs? Your children?

It seems cruel then that
I must crush you
Between my fingers,
Stained brown with bug
Or plant juice — which,
I don't know.

It's a zen teaching:
To abide the ups and downs,
Or so I'm told.
The truth is I am ignorant.
To care for such a life
As *arbor miniscula*

Is art, a balance of freedom
And control. So we wage our war
Of attrition. The browning leaves
And hardening stalk the backdrop
Of our battles and the ticking clock
I race to revive.

You will win, I fear,
And I am gracious in defeat:

I will not begrudge your victory,
But where will you go?
The lifeless husk is trash-bound,
You can't make a home there.

Pyrrhus has advice for you.
Your army multiplies
But your prize is scorched.
No one wins: a shame,
We could have been friends
If you had left my toy alone.

James P. Daigler is an emerging writer of short fiction, essays, and poetry. Communication, storytelling, and humanity's impact on the world are common themes in his work. When not writing, James is an English teacher in Madison, WI, working to inspire the next generation of readers and writers.

You Night - Gabriela Marie Milton

I learned how to read in the mint forest under a pale October moon.

My eyes, blueberries mama gathered in her wicker basket.

The unassuaged yearnings of a golden autumn spread under my skin.

I found the rivers where fish were born, and nightingales sang.

I thought to myself: you, night, how beautiful you are crowned with black poppies and nursing ancient lovers at your chest.

A boat sailed straight through my heart.

The earth stretched its arms to pick up stars.

Then a war started.

A bat-eyed wind blew, and the earth turned toward itself.

And I thought to myself: you night, how painful you are.

Tell me something after I die and before tomorrow's departure.

Let me wear twelve sage leaves on my lips.

Let my body blossom on the Hill of Slane when the breath of sleep rises from the empty crypt.

You night, how wise you are.

Gabriela Marie Milton is an Amazon bestselling poet and an internationally published author. She is the author of the #1 best selling poetry collection Woman: Splendor and Sorrow: | Love Poems and Poetic Prose, and the author of Passions: Love Poems and Other Writings. Gabriela is also the editor of MasicadoresUSA. Her poetry and short prose have appeared in various magazines and anthologies. Under the pen name Gabriela M she was awarded 2019 Author of the Year at Spillwords Press (NYC). Her piece "If I say I love you" was nominated for 2020 Spillwords Press Publication of the Year (Poetic). On July 6, 2021, Gabriela was featured in New York Glamour Magazine.

Stealth - Anne Pinkerton

The deer traffic here,
in from the forest,
with their delicate yet considerable bodies,
they cross, stepping soundlessly through camp,
as if possessing some magic

Over mounds of brown dry leaves,
the litter of fallen branches
without a crunch or snap, without even a sigh

Though the dog occasionally catches
a whiff, her snout arching upward, on the air —
apparently they have a scent, undetectable
to me, nose-blind.

Their single file hoofsteps have pressed
bruised lines into green shoots,
a path of tracks gives them away,
leading to shady spots under purple blossoms,
where I imagine their hidden fawns,
like baby birds tucked into ground nests,
secret snowy spots on their fur
matching the sun-dappled forest floor.

They become accustomed, after time,
to my face, my curiosity, my wide eyes.
We have a staring contest as
one waits a long time to take, carefully,
her next bite of leaf.

They hide in the shadows,
turn a gentle look at me

with some trust and some distrust —
an understanding as fleeting as
the white tail that follows the tawny flanks
camouflaged within the tapestry of leaves
into the blackness of the woods.

All day
I sense the deer
with a sense that is unnamed
private and obscure,
like a secret kept.

Anne Pinkerton studied poetry at Hampshire College and received an MFA in creative nonfiction from Bay Path University. Her writing has been published in Sunlight Press, Hippocampus Magazine, River Teeth's 'Beautiful Things,' Entropy Magazine, Modern Loss, and Ars Medica, among others. Her memoir will be published by Vine Leaves Press in 2023.

Neighborhood Sound - Seth Kronick

mid-autumn
the sound of leaves
sloshing underfoot

mid-autumn
the sound of birds
chirping overhead

mid-autumn
the sound of the breeze
passing all around

mid-autumn
the sound of the boulevard
revving ahead

mid-autumn
the sound of neighbors
cleaning about

mid-autumn
the sound of the
neighborhood

Seth Kronick was born in Goshen, New York before moving to Southern California at the age of ten. While growing up, his passion for poetry and use of imagery has allowed him to thrive while learning from the greats such as Robert Frost, Jack Kerouac, Lewis Carroll, Billy Collins, and Bruce Feingold. Seth is currently studying as an undergraduate student at Fullerton College.

Winter from My Room - Stephen Ruffus

I spread the seed
with a motion like absolution
blessing the birds that come
outside my window,
go inside to wait for them
into the frame
of my narrow sight.

In the distance I can hear
the freight trains clustered
and heavy so they only
shift back and forth
back and forth with a sound
that echoes in your heart.

A church bell plays its music.
It does not play for me
and the music itself
does not stir me
but I am moved nonetheless
that I can hear it at all,
music playing in the street
where it almost never is.

It is snowing.
The birds have spread
over the ground
searching for
what lies underneath.
I step into another room
only to return

and find them gone
leaving me to dwell
alone with my hunger.

Stephen Ruffus's work has appeared or is forthcoming in the Valparaiso Poetry Review, the American Journal of Poetry, Eunoia Review, Red Eft Review, The Stray Branch, Hotel Amerika, Vita Brevis, and The Shore. He has studied poetry at Colorado State University, the University of California at Irvine, and the University of Utah. He is from New York City and resides in Salt Lake City.

Mulberries in the Piedmont
- Bartholomew Barker

From the first snow melt
until my coatless hike,
I've walked under this tree
without noticing its mulberries.

I rush to pluck the fruit,
ripened purple over a warm night,
pop juicy morsels in my stained mouth,
gambling on sweet against tart.

A mother starling nags from overhead,
so I leave a few for her hatchlings —
a generosity I now regret.

Mulberry season is precarious —
and a man can't be held responsible
in these perilous times.

Bartholomew Barker is an organizer of Living Poetry, a collection of poets in North Carolina. Born and raised in Ohio, studied in Chicago, he worked in Connecticut for nearly twenty years before moving to Hillsborough where he makes money as a computer programmer to fund his poetry habit. bartbarkerpoet.com

Revelation - Kelly Sargent

Beside my cabin, a reflection shimmers
on humid luminescence
that bewitches me curiously within,
captivating me against my will.

The brazen luster measures without apology
my depths and my shallows
without my consent,
revealing secrets I've kept surreptitiously hidden
from sunlight

that continues to remain loyal
whether I deserve it or not.

Entranced in a mesmeric gaze, we eye one another
uneasily
until a dragonfly skims the surface
and breaks the enchantment.
I am revealed in ripples that disseminate
an imperfect nature.

An emerging poet and artist this year, Kelly Sargent's poems and artwork, including a current "Best of the Net" nominee, appeared or are forthcoming in more than two dozen literary publications in 2021. Her debut poetry chapbook entitled "Seeing Voices: Poetry in Motion" is also forthcoming (Kelsay Books, 2022). She serves as Creative Nonfiction Editor of The Bookends Review, as well as a reviewer for Awakened Voices, a literary magazine dedicated to making visible the artistic expression of sexual violence survivors.

A pioneer. - DS Maolalai

and we used to have
this problem
although it wasn't really
a problem:

wake up to breakfast,
and to patterns
on the tile. the snails got in
at night, according
to my grandmother – it was warmer
than outside
and I guess they sheltered
there. tracing shapes
like shining crayon,
you could track them
if you wanted. I was a kid –
interested in animals –
I did.

over the doormat
and along the tile, I found
adventures. snails coming
to this new place
which must have seen
so obscure. exploring – finding just
this alien area. and fleeing.
the trail always lead
back outside.

but sometimes,
just occasionally,
you'd find

a pioneer. dry on the tile
in the center
like an old walnut
shell. a hero.
my mother
would throw him out again, to break
and shine in the soil. now
when I visit
I leave the heat on at night
plus there's a brush
I bolted to the door.

no adventures
anymore.
no mopping
after breakfast.

DS Maolalai has been nominated nine times for Best of the Net and seven times for the Pushcart Prize. His poetry has been released in two collections, "Love is Breaking Plates in the Garden" (Encircle Press, 2016) and "Sad Havoc Among the Birds" (Turas Press, 2019)

Tenacity - Sherry Poff

Against all odds on a bright afternoon,
snow lingers in the shadows, skulks
in corners and the shelter of a tree.
Yesterday's white maiden
a wizened crone,
doing what she must to survive.

Sherry Poff writes in and around Ooltewah, Tennessee. She holds an M.A. in writing from The University of Tennessee at Chattanooga and is a member of the Chattanooga Writers' Guild. Her work has appeared recently in Raconteur Review, Heart of Flesh, *and* The Chattanooga Pulse.

Witness of the Unseen - Catherine

Now too much sun,
and lovely is its lope,
I tried on the corner,
stood - the making of
a monument looking out
at the garden spilling
gardenias too bright
a white to be seen,
yet they spoke such
a scent, all grief was
swept from the heart,
no one had died, nor
would they ever

Catherine is a published poet living in New England. Her works have appeared in Atlas Poetica, hedgerow, Moonbathing, various anthologies and elsewhere in Africa, India, Japan, the United Kingdom and the United States.

Sidewalk Gallery - Ali Grimshaw

a recent fallen member
of the Past Their Prime Club
rests gracefully in the colored collective
with crinkle smoked wrinkles of a life lived large

beaten by winds of circumstance
veins of strength unwilling to release
what is left of delicate steadfastness
now fallen to land in vulnerability

no longer sheltered by limbs arched above
touched by vibrant shine of still glow
and flame of Autumn illumination
beauty's full circle displayed

on wet cement

Ali Grimshaw contributes to the world as an educator, life coach, and poet. Her poems have been published in several anthologies and journals including, Vita Brevis, Right Hand Pointing, Visual Verse, and Ghost City Review. You can find her writing circle offerings and her poetry at flashlightbatteries.blog.

Toward the Wild - Chris Wood

Shadows lake across the night,
paws roaming, weaving adventure
in new-found freedom.

Coyotes howl, possums hide
behind the darkness.
Spiders web the porch lights,
spinning laid eggs for incubation.

Corncrakes sing while stars pillow
my dreams. False summer warms
a trail worn by fawns
and neighborhood children,
both growing, seeking independence.

Lost in a labyrinth of suburban landscape,
moonlight pools between pine
and cedar fences. Scents guide, enthrall,
draw him closer to nature,
leading him to a pathway
connecting to his roots.

Chris Wood resides in Tennessee with her husband and several fur babies. Her work has appeared in several journals and publications, including Poetry Quarterly, Haiku Journal, American Diversity Report, *and* Quill and Parchment.

Renewed - Ray Zimmerman

The breeze stirs leaf and branch to life.
They gossip of coming rainfall.

The waterfall is nearly silent,
but a storm grows in the west.
It will sing with a booming voice.

Fungal networks lie dormant
in dry earth, but soon awaken
and carry messages from tree to tree.

Maples go from green to yellow
and yellow to red, but sometimes
remain half changed, undecided.

I lie asleep, but sunrise approaches.
Will the newborn sun revive me too,
prepared to seize the dawning day?

Ray Zimmerman has edited the Chattanooga Writers' Guild Newsletter. Nonfiction works include articles in the Chattanooga Pulse, Appalachian Voices (Bone, NC), and the Hellbender Press (Knoxville). Poems have appeared in The Avocet, Number One (Gallatin, TN), The Southern Poetry Anthology, Volume VI, Tennessee (Texas Review Press)., and other fine journals. □

Visitor - Elizabeth Barton

An errant blackbird with gliding hop
darts across my view, as neatly as a wave
unwrapping a lazy ocean, as beguiling
as remembered music;
he stops for buried worms; and time
pauses in the tilt of his head; with buoyant grace
he enlivens the air, lightly springing with coiled joy
he textures the ground he touches, his fluid form
effortless. I pause and listen too,
for the miracle within his world.

Elizabeth Barton is an artist and poet from New Zealand, with work featured in Pink Plastic House, Spillwords, Fevers of the Mind, Black Bough Poetry's Rapture, and Winter/Christmas Edition 2021. A winner of the White Label Cinq poetry competition in 2020, she has a collection soon to be published with Hedgehog Poetry Press.

Twilight - Elizabeth Barton

Twilight falls, a brooding damask rose
ruing the loss of her bloom;
heady fragrance of dying day drifts
nostalgic on stolen evening air.

Night intrudes with velvet stealth,
its long black boots tread the contours
of gully and hill, trailing a cloak
of shadows, footfall of ashen petals.

Layered darkness descends, the folds
of yesterday's newspapers in rain-washed grey
hang weightless in the fading light,
remembered in the roll of dusked valleys,
mute sombre outline of land on sky,
last burnished flush divides air and earth.

Elizabeth Barton is an artist and poet from New Zealand, with work featured in Pink Plastic House, Spillwords, Fevers of the Mind, Black Bough Poetry's Rapture, and Winter/Christmas Edition 2021. A winner of the White Label Cinq poetry competition in 2020, she has a collection soon to be published with Hedgehog Poetry Press.

Lach di Ciàz - Alessio Zanelli

Foot after foot
the peaks emerge
from the forest.

My ghost awakes
and rises up,
above the trees,
above the crest
of aging dreams.

My eyes command
what used to rule
my head below,
but not the heights,
the upper heights
of yore of which
I must let go.

Let go to go.

Alessio Zanelli is an Italian poet who writes in English. His work has appeared in nearly 200 literary journals from 16 countries. His fifth original collection, titled The Secret Of Archery, *was published in 2019 by Greenwich Exchange (London). For more information please visit alessiozanelli.it.*

A Door There Was - K Roberts

Above your curtains are curtains and a hush.
Here a serene disciple, there a secret fear
Conceived within the bed of wilderness.
Pyramids of pine, the feverish
Delight that rims the infinite, the sere
Burnt hour and ear of radiance.
Above your curtains are curtains and a hush.

Inside your door a door there was and shut.
The starfish saved in a dusty trunk
Turns the deaf pages of your knock.
The mountain breathes through its cavernous gill
A gong in the sky, the indelible moon.
A threshold is a mischief in a wood.
Inside your door a door there was and shut.

K Roberts is a professional non-fiction writer and artist who also publishes poetry. "A Door There Was" responds to the photograph "Mannequin" by Sal Taylor Kydd. It received a merit award in an ekphrastic challenge, Poetry in Motion, co-hosted by Page Gallery (thepagegallery.com) and Poet's Corner (thepoetscorner.org) of Camden, Maine in autumn 2021.

Winter Tracks of Deer - Judy DeCroce

Light leaves early —
a courtesy to night.
Burning stars above
the newest snow.
How it collects in hollows,
casts its cage way past fall.
A young deer stumbles distracted
then hurries to follow.
These faithful shadows tread slowly
surrendering to the white —
And the sky too, bends,
following tracks.

Judy DeCroce lives and works in rural upstate New York with her husband, poet/artist, Antoni Ooto. She is a poet, flash fiction writer and professional storyteller. Judy is widely published globally in print, online, and in anthologies.

Once - Antoni Ooto

spotted; spindly legged
feeling the joy of play
in and out of the pond;

fawns showing off or faking danger;
insistently untamable sprinting away

once twins,
less than a season old,
this one fallen— lays still,

to winter along the gully
as earth edges her in;

her daily path last crossed,
where she died in the coming chill,

wide-eyed homeward
facing East.

Antoni Ooto lives and works in rural upstate New York with his wife, poet, Judy DeCroce. He is a well-known abstract expressionist painter whose art is collected throughout the US. Currently, poetry is an additional expression of his creativity and widely published globally in print, online, and in anthologies.

All the News - Connie Jordan Green

The wren is building her nest beneath
the eaves—back and forth all day from lawn
and bush, beak filled with construction material.

Above the birdbath, bluebirds line
a maple limb, wait a turn at the shallow
bowl, rainbows splashing in the sunlight.

And in the field crows hunch
from foot to foot, old men in black
disgruntled even on this fine April morning.

It's all the news we need today.

Connie Jordan Green lives on a farm in East Tennessee where she writes and gardens. She is the author of award-winning novels for young people, poetry chapbooks, and two poetry collections. Her poetry has been nominated for Pushcart Prizes. She frequently leads writing workshops.

A Pond - Mark Weinrich

A pond
is a library
of the sky,
where reflections
are collected,
yet sadly
few checked out.
To sky-readers
no matter
how instant
the message,
it flickers
and shines
with jubilation.

Mark Weinrich lives a creative life as a writer, photographer, musician, and artist — all wrapped together in an outdoorsman. He is a retired pastor and nine-year cancer survivor. His writing and photography have appeared in over 135 news stand, inspirational, and literary publications. He has sold eight children's books.

Spirit Suite Étude N° 12 - Lorraine Caputo

I lay in the clear green water
between the driftwood
& reef
Floating like seagrass
anchored at my arms
amongst the seaweed
My leg-blades sway
with each wash
of the waves

& when I emerge
my skin tightens
in the warm afternoon
Shelldust clings
to my toes
& palms

Poet-translator Lorraine Caputo's works appear in over 300 journals on six continents; and 19 collections of poetry – including On Galápagos Shores *(dancing girl press). Her work has been nominated for the Best of the Net Award. She journeys through Latin America, listening to the voices of the pueblos and Earth.*

Made in the USA
Las Vegas, NV
25 January 2022

42312733R00100